White House of Confederacy — Montgomery, Ala.

To
The people of Montgomery this book is dedicated. They have cooperated with us in our efforts to improve the cultural and welfare facilities of our city for the past twenty-seven years.
    The Montgomery Junior League
            1956

— Table of Contents —

Cocktails - pg - 4

Canapés and Sandwiches - pg. 11

Soups - pg. 23

Sea Foods - pg. 38

Luncheon Dishes - pg. 54

Poultry and Game - pg. 76

Meat and Fish Sauces - pg. 94

Meats - pg. 101

Vegetables - pg. 117

Salads and Salad Dressings - pg 146

Breads - pg. 169

Desserts - pg 187

Cakes - Cookies - Icings - pg. 229

Candies - pg. 276

Preserves and Pickles - pg. 285

Beverages - pg. 298

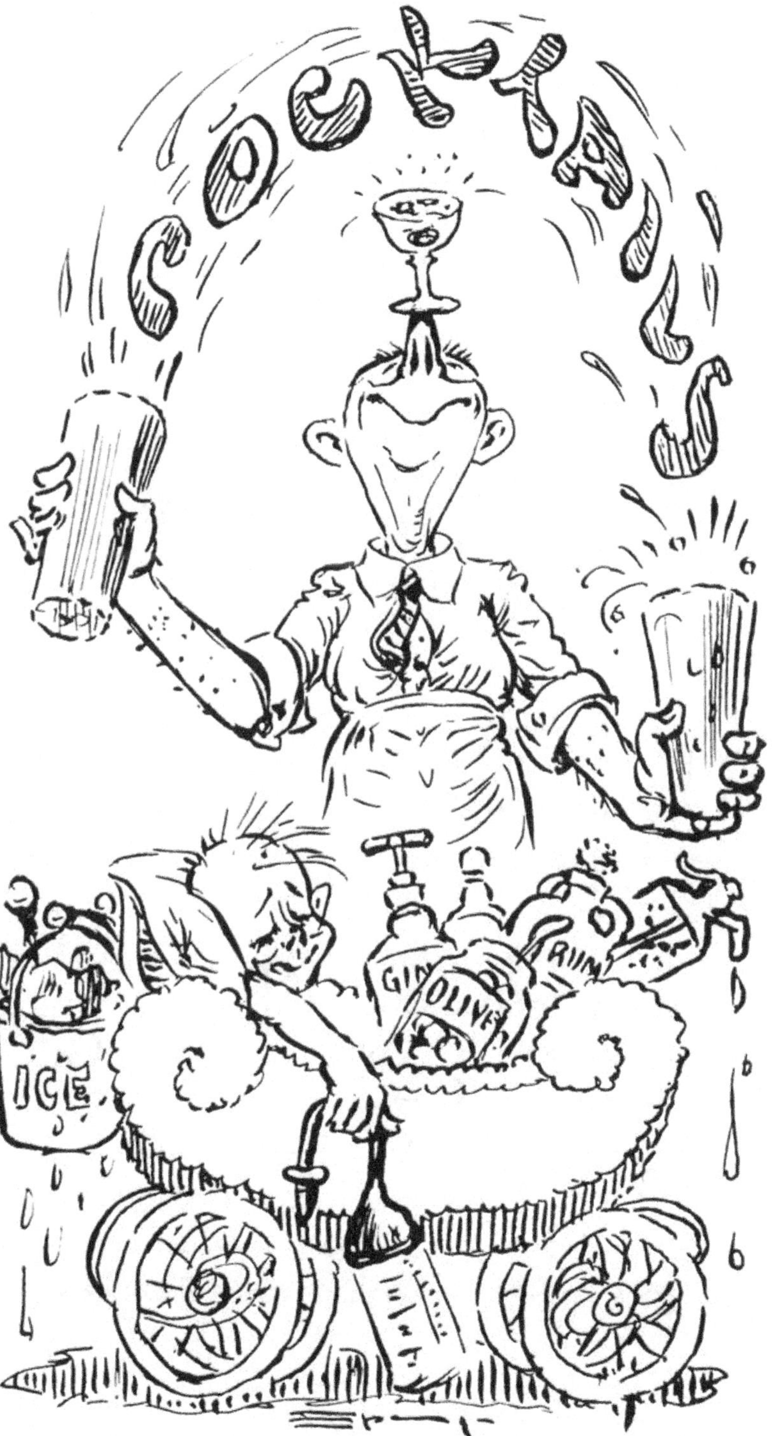
COCKTAILS
ICE
GIN
OLIVE
RUM

Christmas Egg Nog

5 quarts milk
1 quart cream
2 dozen eggs
½ dozen egg whites
nutmeg
1½ qts. whiskey
sugar to taste

Separate eggs. Beat yolks until thick. Beat whites until stiff. Whip cream. Whip milk. Add everything separately. When ready to serve fold in whites. Sprinkle nutmeg over the top as served. This will serve twenty people.

Mrs. Walter Weaver

"Virginia Beach Punch"

(Tastes mild – kicks violently!)

Mix:
Juice of 3 lemons
Peelings (not pulp) of 3 lemons
2 water glasses Whiskey
1 water glass water
1 cup sugar

Leave for 24 hours. Strain. Chill before serving and do not add ice. This mixture can be kept indefinitely, growing more potent each day.

— Mrs. Wiley Hill, Jr.

— Egg Nog —

1 qt. Cream   2 glasses Whiskey
13 eggs   1 glass Rum

Beat yellows until stiff – add 1 lb. sugar and whip like meringue. Whip 1 qt. Cream. Mix in order: yolks, whiskey, whites of eggs, cream. Serves 12.

— Mrs. Michael Microsi

Whiskey Sour

2 qts. Bourbon whiskey
1 qt. lemon juice and rind
1 pt. sugar syrup
1 teaspoonful lemon extract

      Mrs. Walter Weaver
        Maxwell Field

Dixie Punch

1 gal. strong cold tea
2 doz. lemons
small amount sugar
2 qts. ginger ale

    add 1 pt. good whiskey
to 1 gal. of above mixture.

      Mrs. Henry D. Clayton

Mint Julep

Few sprigs of mint
Finely crushed ice
Sugar
Bourbon or Rye whiskey

Place in tall glass or julep cup one heaping teaspoonful of sugar. Add to this a drop or two of water or just enough to melt sugar. Into this pack ice, leaving about half an inch at top. Pour over ice 1 jigger of bourbon or rye whiskey. With ice tea spoon frappé or stir hard this mixture for several seconds until frost begins to appear on outside of glass. Top with crushed ice and a sprig of mint. Serve with straws.

Mrs. Olwi Stokes.

Blue Moon Cocktails

6 oranges   1 teaspoon sugar
6 lemons   pinch of salt
          dash of bitters
9 jiggers of bourbon and shake with ice.

          Miss Leila Clowe

Mint Cocktails

1½ jiggers gin
½ jigger lime juice
½ jigger lemon juice
1 teaspoon sugar
leaves from 2 stalks of mint
few drops creme de menthe to color. Crush mint & sugar with fruit juice. Add gin. Strain & serve in cocktail glass with shaved ice. This makes one drink.

          Mrs. H. D. Houghton

Twenty-four Hour Cocktail

1 doz. lemons — juice and rind.
4 cups whisky — 4 cups water
1 cup sugar.

Add lemon juice with rind of lemons, and water, whiskey, and sugar. Let stand 24 hours — stirring often. Strain, and serve chilled.

      Mrs. Spencer Longshore.

Sherbet for Cocktails

3/4 cups sugar — juice 2 oranges
1 cup water — juice 2 lemons
4 bottles of 7-up.

Freeze ingredients to mush in refrigerator tray. Fill cocktail glasses with sherbet. Pour over each glass 1 jigger of whiskey.

      Mrs. G. C. Youngerman.

Orange Blossom

Juice of 3/4 of an orange
1 tsp. sugar — 1 jigger gin

Pour this mixture in a cocktail glass. Fill the glass with crushed ice, and serve.

hors d'oeuvres

Jane Troy Hooker

Cheese Loaf

¼ lb. New York State cheese
¼ lb. cream cheese
¼ lb. pimento cheese
¼ lb. pecans

Put all ingredients through meat grinder. Mix well and season with salt, red pepper, lemon juice, chopped onion & Worcestershire sauce. Shape into a roll slightly smaller than a Ritz cracker. Sprinkle paprika on wax paper and roll up cheese. Put in refrigerator to harden. When cold, slice and serve on crackers.

  Mrs. James L. Screws

A Man's Sandwich

1 package Philadelphia Cream Cheese - Blend well and add one beaten egg yolk - 1 tsp. grated onion pulp, salt, and pepper to taste. Spread on rounds of bread and run in hot oven.

Mrs. Edward Gresham -

Cream Cheese Mixture

(for "dunking" potato chips)
1 package Philadelphia cream cheese softened with cream. Season with dash of grated garlic and some grated onion (to taste) - adding also, a few drops at a time, ½ tsp. Worcestershire sauce, salt, and paprika. Mixture should be of the consistency of whipped cream.

Mrs. Arthur Mead -

Toasted Bread Cups with Cheese

Use bakery rolls about 4 inches long, cut in half and scooped out in center. Fill with the following mixture: American cheese grated and mixed with mayonnaise, a little Worcestershire sauce, a little mustard. Toast and serve very hot. (cooked sausage may be used as a filling.)

Mrs. Frank H. Miller

Anchovy Appetizers

Make a rich pastry dough. Roll out and cut with small biscuit cutter. Spread about an inch or more of anchovy on one corner. Roll this into small ball and pinch together. Fry in deep fat and put on brown paper to cool.

Majorie Allen

Canapé

1/3 cup mayonnaise   1 cup minced tuna fish
3 tbsp. prepared horseradish   salt to taste.

Mix thoroughly and spread on cracker or cocktail biscuit.

Mrs. H. S. Haughton

Bacon Canapé

Wrap slices of bacon around Snowflake crackers, using one piece of bacon to each cracker. Put in biscuit pan & place under flame for bacon to cook. Watch carefully as they burn quickly.

Mrs. Perry Thomas.

Canapé

½ cup deviled ham
1 teaspoon chopped pickle
12 small mushrooms sautéd
Spread ham and pickle on crackers. Top each one with one mushroom.

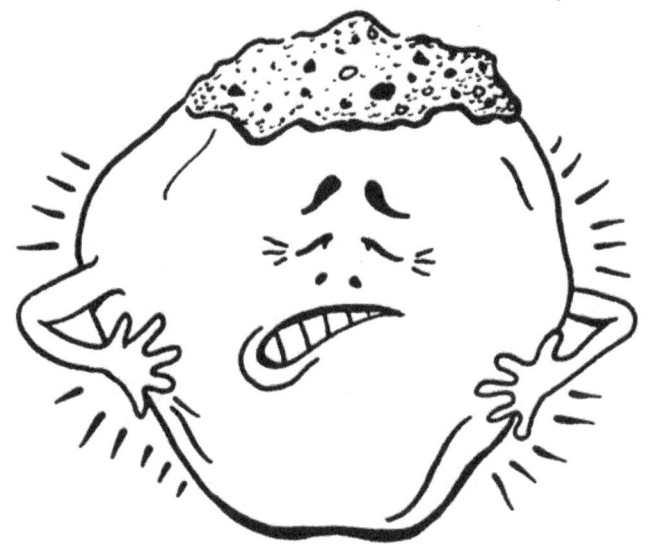

      Mrs. C. W. Hooper
        Selma, Alabama

Stuffed Green Pepper Canapé

1 Philadelphia Cream Cheese
a little sweet cream
chopped pecans
A very little dry mustard
Salt

Mix well — stuff in green pepper, then put on ice for several hours. Slice thin and serve on crackers.

      Eleanor Freeborn Graves

Cheese Biscuits

½ lb. American cheese
½ lb. butter
½ lb. (2 cups) White Lily flour

Cream all together in a cool place, roll 1/8 in. thick. Brush tops in beaten whole egg, sprinkle with ground nuts. Bake in moderately quick oven until brown.

    Miss Leila Dove

Cheese Straws

2 cups N. Y. state cheese
½ cup butter
1½ cups White Lily flour
1 level teasp. baking powder
Salt and pepper to taste

Cream butter and grated cheese. Sift baking powder with White Lily flour. Add seasoning and knead all together. Fill cookie cutter and press out into designs. Bake in a moderate oven.

    Mrs. Thomas H. Edwards

1,000 Island Sandwiches

1 pound New York State cheese, grated.
1 cup chili sauce
1 medium size bottle of stuffed olives (cut up)
2 green peppers - chopped fine
1 large onion (juice)
1 cup of pecans (broken fine)
2 slices of bacon (broiled)
1½ cups mayonnaise.
2 tablespoons Worcestershire sauce.
Salt and pepper.

Mix all together and spread on whole wheat or white bread. Also good to stuff tomatoes with

Mrs. Jack Noll

17.

Sandwich Loaf

Take 1 loaf unsliced bread, remove crusts and cut into fine lengthwise slices. Make a mixture of minced hard boiled eggs, relish, and deviled ham. Butter bread with mayonnaise and ham mixture, laying slice on slice to reshape loaf. Take one package Knox gelatine, and soften with a little water. Heat 1 can Campbell's tomato soup with a small onion. Add to gelatine, allowing hot soup to melt gelatine. Put bowl of soup in bowl of ice to set. When soup begins to thicken ice entire loaf, and garnish with sliced ripe olives. Put in ice box to set.

Mrs. A. J. Cassels, Sr.

Shrimp Sandwiches

½ lb. shrimp (cooked)
juice of 1 lemon
mayonnaise to soften
5 or 6 tender pieces of celery
Salt and pepper to taste

Grate or grind shrimp, cut celery in very small pieces, and add to shrimp. Add lemon juice, salt, pepper, and enough mayonnaise to spread easily. Makes about 12 sandwiches.

Mrs. J. B. Hill, Jr.

Egg Sandwiches —

1 dozen Eggs —
1 package Chipped Beef —
2 medium size Onions — grated
1 cup mayonnaise — highly seasoned —
season with prepared mustard, salt and
pepper. Hard boil eggs. Put them
through sieve or small grater. Crisp
chipped beef in butter and drain
on brown paper. Combine eggs, beef,
mayonnaise, onions and seasoning.
Spread thin sliced bread with more
mayonnaise before using filling.

— Mrs. Teague Rainer —

— Cheese Toasties —

Cut bread round with biscuit cutter.
Put melted butter, grated cheese, nuts
(pecans) and 3 or 4 drops of
Worcestershire sauce on each slice.
Toast in stove until light brown and
crisp. Serve while hot.

— Mrs. John Kohn, Sr.

For Special Recipes

For Special Recipes

Cheese Balls

½ cup grated American cheese
1 tsp. flour
¼ tsp. salt
Cayenne pepper to taste.

Mix well. Add three egg whites beaten stiff. Shape into balls. Roll in cracker crumbs. Fry in deep fat, and drain on brown paper.

Serves eight.

Mrs. Bert C. Weil

Soups fit for a King

23-

Blackeye Pea Soup

1 pt. peas
1 tbsp. chopped onions
1 tsp. chopped green pepper
3 pts. water
3 strips bacon

Broil bacon, sauté onions and pepper in grease. Shred bacon and add with onions and pepper to peas and water. Cook slowly for about 3 hrs. Run through sieve, mashing peas thoroughly. Add 1 cup light cream or milk, salt to taste and serve with 1 inch squares of very dry toast.

   Mrs. H. S. Houghton

Green Split Pea Soup

1 ham hock
1 pound split peas
8 onions (medium size)
nutmeg
1 1/2 lemons

Cook together 4 hours, strain and add 3 hard boiled eggs. Season with La Rosa sherry wine.

   Mrs. Churchill Marks

Cream of Mushroom Soup

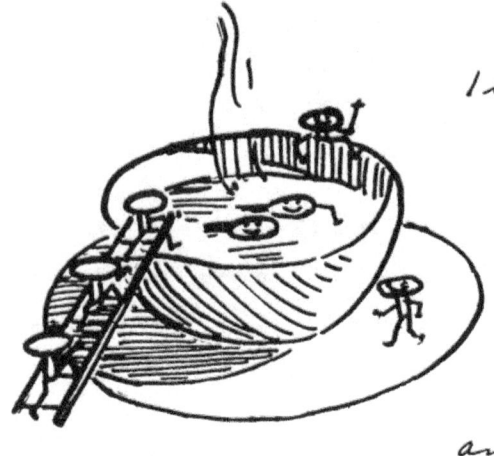

1 lb. fresh mushrooms
1 qt. cream
1 T. butter
Salt to taste

Boil mushrooms in small amount of water until tender. Save stock. Grind mushrooms, add stock, cream, salt and butter. Cook in double boiler. Serves six.

   Mrs. James Fitts Hill

Ham Soup

½ pound raw ham ⎫
6 raw carrots   ⎬ ground
3 onions   ⎭
2 cans tomatoes
½ teaspoon sugar
1 teaspoon powdered sugar
2 quarts water
Salt and pepper

Cook until quite thick. Serves ten.

   Mrs. Henry Crenshaw

White Soup with Wine

4 lbs. knuckle of veal	Bit of bay leaf
2 qts. cold water	1 tbsp. salt
3 carrots sliced	Few grains cayenne
1 onion sliced	1/2 tsp. pepper corn
4 stalks celery	2 tbsp. La Rosa
2 sprigs parsley	Sauterne wine
1 tsp. beef extract	1 cup cream

Wipe meat, remove from bone and cut in small pieces. Put meat and bone in soup kettle, cover with water and add carrots, onion, celery, parsley, bay leaf, salt, cayenne and pepper corn. Bring quickly to boiling point, simmer 5 hrs. and strain. Chill, remove fat, reheat, add La Rosa wine, beef extract and cream. Season with salt and cayenne.

Mrs. Files Crenshaw

Jellied 'Consomme'

2 lbs. veal knuckles
1 lb. lean beef
Salt and pepper
Bay leaves - water
Boil down and when cooked let stand to cool. Skim off grease. Reheat to serve hot with whipped cream. Make day before to serve cold and jellied with paprika or lemon slice.

   Mrs Weldon W. Doe

Tomato Bouillon

1 can beef bouillon
2 cups tomato juice
2 slices onion
1 bay leaf
3 cloves
½ teaspoon celery salt or celery leaves
salt and pepper to taste
2 hard boiled eggs.

 Put all ingredients (except eggs) in saucepan. Simmer gently for thirty minutes.

Then strain through cheese cloth. Serve hot with slices of egg in each cup.

Mrs. R. S. Hill

=Camp Stew=

2 lbs. lean fresh pork
1 qt. canned tomatoes
1 ½ t. corn
1 pt. ground onions
2 cans Campbell's Tomato Soup.

Boil pork 'til tender. Cool and grind. Take broth (1 quart of it), add meat and other ingredients. Cook until thickness desired, stirring constantly. Season with Worcestershire Sauce, tomato catsup, salt and pepper.

Mrs. Fannie L. Oliver

Crab Gumbo

1 4 lb. hen	1 lb. okra
1 small soup or ham bone	1 bay leaf
2 lbs. fresh shrimp	1 onion
1 lb. dark crab meat	1 teas. salt
1 qt. oysters	1 small clove garlic
1 can tomatoes	dash of black & red pepper

Boil ham or soup bone with bay leaf, salt & pepper. Remove bones & cook hen in stock until tender. Remove bones of chicken.

Alice McG. Ledbetter

In another boiler, boil shrimp that have been skinned & cleaned. Remove shrimp from water and cook 2 cups of rice in shrimp water. Add 1 onion cooked in Wesson oil with 1 can tomatoes.

Cut up okra fine and add. When tender add crab meat, oysters and shrimp. Let boil 5 mins. or until oysters are plump. Serve in soup plates with rice that has been cooked in shrimp water.

    Mrs. C.K. Duncan Sr.

Jellied Tomato Consommé

½ can Tomatoes 1 cup raw carrots
1 bay leaf 2 small onions chopped
6 cloves salt, pepper to taste
celery chopped (leaves + stalks)
1 Can Campbell's Consommé Madrilene

Cook above ingredients to-gether until carrots are tender. Steam slowly, add 1 tablespoon Worcestershire sauce, 1 teaspoon lemon juice. Strain + add 2 cans White Rose Consommé. Put in refrigerator for 12 hrs.

   Mrs. Sam Rice Baker

Shrimp Bisque

1 qt. milk -
1 pt. cream (an extra ½ pt. whipped and added with a sprig of parsley to each bowl when served)
¼ lb. butter
4 slightly rounded tbsp White Lily flour -
1 can Campbell's Tomato Soup -
1½ lbs. cooked shrimp - or 3 lb. raw shrimp (the raw shrimp preferred when cooked 20 min. in highly seasoned water)
2 cups La Rosa sherry wine
1 tbsp. Worcestershire sauce
1 tbsp. Lemon juice -
Salt - and tabasco to taste

Melt butter and add flour - cook 5 minutes. When smooth - add milk - then tomato soup, then cream. Add shrimp.

Ten minutes before serving, add sherry, lemon juice, and Worcestershire sauce. After shrimp has been added - do not cook - just keep hot. Serves 10.

Mrs. Temple Seibels

New Orleans Oyster Stew

1 large onion, chopped fine —
1/4 cup parsley, " very fine —
1/4 lb. butter —
1 tbsp. Worcestershire Sauce —
Salt, pepper, cayenne, chili powder
                                to taste —
1 qt. Oysters with liquor —
1 1/2 qts. milk —
1/2 cup finely ground Cracker Crumbs —

Sauté chopped onions and parsley in butter. Add seasonings. Add strained liquor from oysters. Stir constantly to keep from curdling. Add oysters and simmer until edges curl. Meantime have milk heating slowly until scalded. Add above mixture to milk and heat thoroughly. When ready to serve, add cracker crumbs and stir well. Fill soup plates with about 6 oysters to each, then add stew. Sprinkle top with paprika and serve.

   Mrs. Jewell Wheeler
   Maxwell Field, Ala.

Pea Hull Soup

Cover pea hulls with water and boil until tender. Strain and to each cup of liquid add 1 cup milk. Thicken with White Lily flour and add 1 tbsp. butter. Season with salt, pepper and paprika to taste. Add 1 small onion and simmer 5 minutes. Remove onion and serve hot.

   Mrs. James M. Scott
   Scotia, Ala.

Onion Soup

4 onions sliced very thin
1 tablespoon White Lily flour
½ cup grated Parmesan cheese
4 oz. butter
2 oz. La Rosa wine (white)
1 qt. chicken or beef stock
2 sliced toasted rolls or bread

Fry onions in butter until slightly brown; add White Lily flour and stir well; add La Rosa wine and meat stock. Allow to boil 15 min. Salt and pepper to taste. Put in bowls with slices of toasted bread. Spread cheese on top, then bake in hot oven until brown.

Ella Baggs Graves

Clear Tomato Soup

1 large can of whole tomatoes
Equal amount of water
1 tbsp. butter - sprig of celery
Dash of red pepper - slice of onion -
1 bay leaf - 1 tbsp Lea & Perrin sauce -
Juice of a lemon if tomatoes lack acidity.
½ tsp. sugar -   2 tsp. salt -

Mix all ingredients and let simmer for 20 minutes. Strain and serve.

Mrs. Lister Hill -

- Brunswick Stew -

1 hen.   4 ears corn -
2 lbs. pork -   3 medium size potatoes
6 tomatoes - or 2 cans tomatoes
2 cans tomato soup - 1 small onion
1 bottle catsup.

Cook hen and pork separately. Cut meat into small pieces - add to chicken stock. Add other ingredients - also red and black pepper - salt and Worcestershire sauce to taste. Cook over low flame about 2 or 3 hours.

Mrs. J. L. Rouse -

Oyster Bisque

1 pint oysters.
Heat oysters in liquor until tender. Mash oysters thru a sieve. Skim its liquor and add enough sweet milk to make 2 cups of liquid. Heat. While this is heating, take 2 tablespoons of butter and 2 tablespoons of White Lily flour. Blend thoroughly and add liquor. 1½ teaspoons salt, mace, and a few drops of Tabasco. Add oysters and cook slowly until thick. When ready to serve, add 1 beaten egg. 1 cup of cream - or a can of Carnation milk.
    Sprinkle with parsley and paprika.

           Mrs. Michel Nieraei.

Cream of Onion Soup

1 cup chopped onions
½ cup diced celery
3 cups milk
2 tbsp. minced parsley
4 tbsp. butter
1 tbsp. flour
1 egg; salt and pepper

Cook onions, parsley and celery in butter over low fire until tender. Stir in flour and when well blended, add milk, stirring constantly. Bring to boiling point. Let simmer 20 min. Beat egg slightly with 3 tbsp. of cream. Strain soup into egg, stirring vigorously. Cook 2 min. stirring constantly and serve. Serve with Parmesan cheese on top with whipped cream

Mrs. Edwin I. Hatch

Sea Foods

Joe Clancy

Trout Armandine

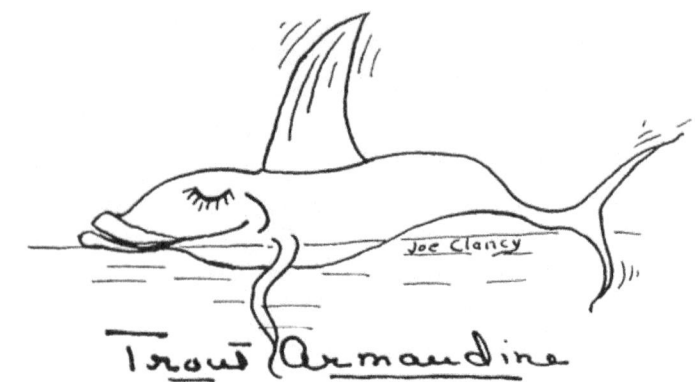

Have butcher bone a trout or any fine-grained fish and cut into serving size pieces. Put in the refrigerator to soak a little while in a little sweet milk. Then drain and dip into seasoned flour to which a dash of baking powder has been added — as for fried chicken. Have lots of butter very hot in a skillet and fry fish until a delicate brown. Then place on a hot platter.

Drop almonds, which have been blanched and coarsely chopped, into butter remaining in the skillet and brown lightly. Pour butter and almonds over the fish and serve. Plenty

of butter must be used and
no water added – use just
the browned butter as gravy.

      Mrs. Floyd McGowin
        Chapman, Alabama

– Lobster á la Newburg –

1½ cups milk
1½ tbsp. butter
1 tbsp. White Lily Flour
Salt and cayenne –
1 tbsp. Worcestershire sauce
Juice and rind of one lemon
Yolks of 2 eggs – well beaten
1 wine glass of La Rosa sherry

Make a white sauce of the first four ingredients. Add Worcestershire sauce, lemon, and egg yolks. When thick, add one pound of lobster meat and the sherry.

      Mrs. Forney Stevenson

Creole Shrimp with Wild Rice

1½ cup wild rice
1 green pepper
1 cup sliced mushrooms
1 small can tomatoes
3 cups shrimp (cooked)
¼ tsp. paprika
salt and pepper to taste
5 tbsp. butter
1 onion
1 tbsp. lemon juice

Wash wild rice free of chaff and cook in usual way. Melt butter in heavy skillet and brown; onion, green pepper, and mushrooms. Add freshly cooked shrimp and cook over hot flame 1 or 2 min. Decrease heat and add 1 small can tomatoes. Cook slowly 5 min., uncovered and stirring constantly. When some of tomato juice has evaporated, lower heat and simmer 10 min. Mold rice in ring. Unmold on a platter and fill center with shrimp mixture.

Mrs. Boyd McGehee

Creamed Shrimp and Green Peas

1 can tiny green peas
1 stick butter
1 cup milk
1 tsp. Worcestershire Sauce
½ lb. cooked shrimp
1 tbsp. White Lily flour

Make a rich cream sauce, using 1 tbsp. White Lily flour to stick of butter. In another boiler have peas and shrimp cooking slowly. Add cream sauce to drained peas and shrimp. Season with salt, pepper, paprika, cut up parsley and Worcestershire sauce. After removing from stove, add La Rosa sherry wine. This receipt may be used with fresh mushrooms instead of shrimp. — Mrs. W. B. Westcott

Deviled Crabs

1 qt. crab meat
1 hard-boiled egg
2 well-beaten eggs
1 cup celery and green peppers mixed
1 Tbsp. lemon juice
3/4 cup mayonnaise
3 Tbsps. Worcestershire sauce
3/4 cups tomato catsup
1 Tbsp. butter
10 crackers, broken fine
1 tsp. mustard
1 tsp. Tabasco sauce
Salt and pepper to taste

Mix all and fill crab shells. Sprinkle cracker crumbs and a dab of butter on top and bake about ½ hour.

Mrs. William Ogg

Joe Clancy

Shrimp Pie

1 lb. boiled shelled shrimp
1 Tbsp. olive oil
1 Tbsp. butter
½ cup Chili Sauce
¼ cup Cream
½ cup coarse bread crumbs
1 Tsp. Worcestershire Sauce
Dash Tabasco or red pepper

Mix ingredients and bake in glass dish for 20 minutes.

Mrs. H.S. Houghton

Crabmeat a la Creole

1 pound Crabmeat
1 medium can tomatoes -
strained and mashed.
1 medium can mushrooms -
chopped.
1 medium can stuffed olives
chopped.
1 bell pepper - chopped
1 stalk celery - chopped
1 small onion - chopped.
1 clove garlic — let stay
in 1 minute
1 tbsp White Lily flour.
2 tbsp Worcestershire sauce
2 tbsp butter - melted
and creamed with flour.
Mold of rice.

    Catherine Dixon

Creamed Crabmeat

1 qt. crab meat
2 tbsp. butter
½ tsp. minced parsley
1 tsp. salt
2 tbsp. White Lily flour
1 egg   1 cup cream
1 pt. sweet milk
1 wine glass of La Rosa
   sherry wine

Smooth butter and flour together. Add milk, cream, egg, salt and pepper. Add crab meat and wine.

   Mrs. David Riley
      Cook.

Oysters in Casserole

2½ qts. large oysters well dried & sprinkled with salt & pepper. Make sauce of:

½ lb. butter   ⅔ tsp. salt
3 tbsp. lemon juice   ⅔ tsp. red pepper
3 tbsp. chopped parsley

Thicken with a little browned flour. Add ½ cup pet milk, and cook a little. If too thick, add more butter. Put oysters in layers in large casserole, & to each layer, add small pieces of bacon cooked to a crisp, sprinkle with cracker crumbs & sauce. Cover last layer with cracker crumbs. Use about 2 cups of cracker crumbs for recipe. This serves 16.

    Mrs. Frank Harvey Miller

Scalloped Oysters

1 pt. oysters
1 1/2 cups milk
grated cheese
cracker crumbs
Salt, pepper, Worcestershire sauce

Let milk come to a boil. Add oysters and cook until the edges curl. Thicken with White Lily flour and water mixture. Add butter, salt, pepper and Worcestershire to taste. Remove from stove. In a casserole arrange layers of oyster mixture, cracker crumbs and cheese. Put in oven long enough for cheese to melt and brown.

Mrs. J. W. Oliver

DEVILED OYSTER

2 cups celery (chopped)
1 cup onions (chopped)
1 quart large oysters (cut in two)
2 tbsp. Lea & Perrins sauce
1 cup tomato catsup.
Salt and pepper.
Bread crumbs.

Brown celery and onions in butter. Add seasoning, butter, bread crumbs. Put a layer of oysters, then a layer of mixture until casserole is filled. Put buttered crumbs on top. Bake 20 minutes in medium oven.

Mrs. Henry Crowsha

Escalloped Tuna

49.

Crumble a 10 cent package of potato chips. Flake a medium sized can of tuna fish. Place these 2 ingredients in layers in a casserole. Pour over this a can of mushroom soup, to which a can of fresh milk has been added. Bake 20 or 25 min. in a moderate oven. Any other sea food may be used.

Miss Mary Ellis

Baked Salmon

2 cans pink salmon
2 lemons
2 tbsp. Worcestershire sauce
1 tbsp. butter
2 tbsp. White Lily flour
2 cups milk
salt and pepper to taste
cracker crumbs

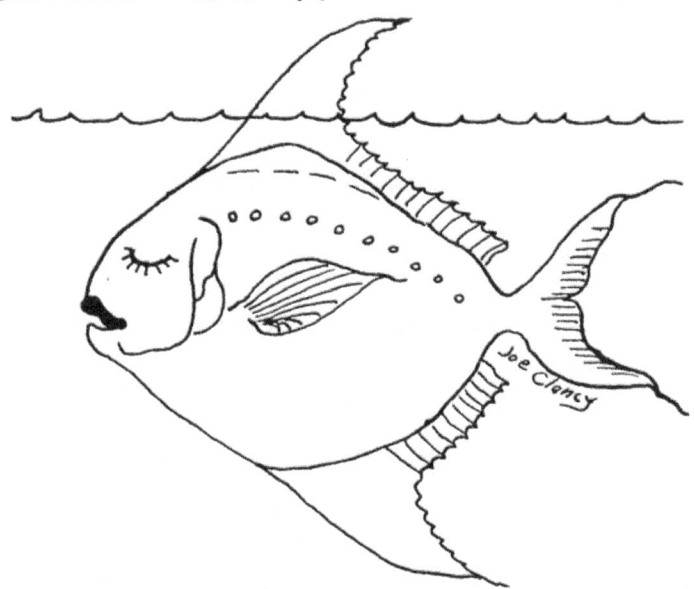

Pick bones from salmon. Mix with juice and grated rind of lemon. Add Worcestershire sauce, salt, and pepper. Make cream sauce of butter, milk, and flour. Add to salmon and mix well. Add cracker crumbs. Put into greased shells. Sprinkle cracker crumbs on top and dot with butter.

Oysters in Shell

3 pints oysters boiled a little in own liquid until they curl

Sauce: 1 cup cream, 1 bottle ketchup (about 1 cup), lemon, lump of butter (size of an egg), worcestershire sauce, salt, pepper.

Let sauce come to a boil, put oysters in shells and baste with sauce continually.

Serves 18 shells.

     Mrs. Bert Evans

Oysters à la Newburg

1 qt. oysters
4 egg yolks
1 pt. cream
1 wine glass La Rosa sherry wine
1 heaping tbsp. butter

Drain oysters, place in double boiler with butter and wine; salt and pepper to taste. Simmer for 5 minutes. Beat egg yolks and add to the cream. Pour over oysters and stir until it thickens. Never boil. Serve on toast.

     Mrs. John Martin

52 -

Fish Mousse

1 large can Salmon, run through very fine strainer. Add gradually 4 slightly beaten egg whites, 1 cup cream, salt, pepper and red pepper. Beat thoroughly and fold in 1 cup whipped cream. Put in buttered mold, cover with buttered paper. Put mold in pan of hot water and bake in moderate oven until firm. Make 2 cups white sauce, pour over the 4 beaten egg yolks, add salt, pepper and 2 Tbsps. La Rosa Sherry wine. Serve sauce separately.

Mrs. Fred Ball, Jr.

Luncheon Suggestions

Hot Tamale Pie

Prepare a mush by stirring 1 cup corn meal with 1 tsp. salt into 3 cups boiling water. Cook in double boiler for about 20 minutes, stirring often. Brown 1 medium size onion, minced, in 1 tbsp. hot bacon fat. Add 1 lb. ground steak. Season with salt and black pepper, then cook a few minutes. Add 1 can Campbell's Tomato soup,

paprika and chili powder to
taste. Grease baking dish
with bacon drippings and
line with cooked noodles. Add
meat mixture and cover with
remainder of noodles. Bake for
1 hour in moderate oven.

    Mrs. C. G. Hume

~ Spaghetti ~

2 lbs. round steak ~
½ lb. raw ham ~
¼ lb. salt pork ~

Have butcher chop the
meat into small cubes, or it can
be coarsely ground.
2 large cans tomatoes
4 large onions ~ chopped or diced ~
4 buttons garlic ~
1 lemon ~ sliced thin ~

56- Put ingredients all together in a steam cooker or other suitable vessel for slow cooking. Season lightly with Lea and Perrin's Sauce, Tabasco, Salt, black and cayenne peppers and cook until meat can be mashed with fork. Remove any surplus fat that you find after mashing. Add 2 cans of tomato paste.

Boil 1 lb. spaghetti (the long Italian kind), drain when tender. Add 1 stick butter to the spaghetti, then pour on the sauce and mix well, being careful not to break the spaghetti. Serve with grated Parmesan or American cheese.

— Mrs. Henry Crenshaw

Chili

1 lb. ground meat (3/4 beef, 1/4 pork)
3 medium onions
1 garlic button

Cut onions and garlic fine, cook meat, onion, and garlic thoroughly in 1/4 cup butter

Add: 2 cans kidney beans
1 can tomatoes (large)
3 tbsp. chili powder
2 tbsp. sugar

Cook slowly in deep boiler. It requires long cooking and much stirring.

    Mrs. Mae Barnes

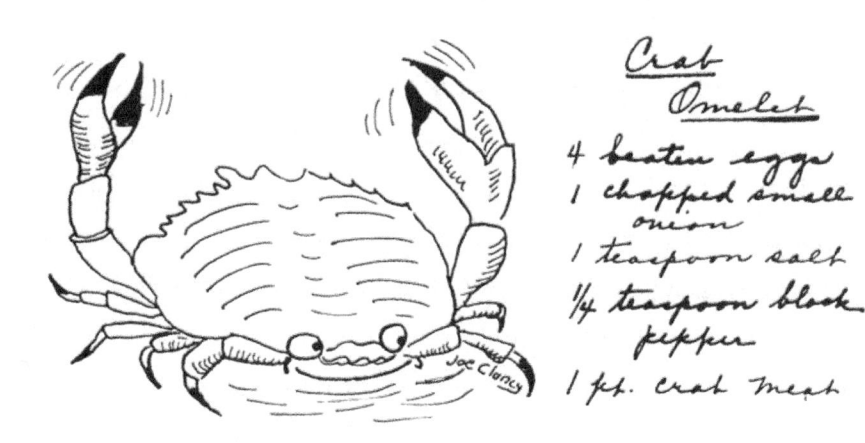

Crab Omelet

4 beaten eggs
1 chopped small onion
1 teaspoon salt
1/4 teaspoon black pepper
1 lb. crab meat

Fry in butter into small omelets. Serve between very hot toasted buns.

    Mrs. John A. Martin

Brain Croquettes

Clean 1 set of brains and let stand in cold water for about 10 min. Put into 1 pt. of boiling water to which has been added 1 tbsp. salt and 1 tbsp. lemon juice. Boil 10 minutes; drain, and pour cold water over them. Let cool - and chop fine; then add ½ cup cracker crumbs, parsley, 1 tbsp. butter, yolks of 5 hard-boiled eggs, and enough cream to soften. Mash - and mix butter, eggs, and other ingredients. Salt and pepper to taste. Roll in cracker crumbs and fry to a golden brown. Serve with mushroom sauce.

Mushroom Sauce

1½ heaping tbsp. White Lily flour
1 tbsp. butter - ½ small onion
Wine glass vinegar - cayenne pepper
1 tsp. sugar - 1 tsp. salt
1 tsp. mustard - 1 can tomatoes
1 can mushrooms
1 tsp. Worcestershire sauce

Cook tomatoes and onions until tender, and mash through a strainer. Add other ingredients and boil.

Mrs. William Off -

Baked Italian Spaghetti

2 lbs. round steak (sliced) - 1 lemon -
3 cans #2 tomatoes - 2 medium green peppers
1 small can tomato sauce - 1 bud garlic
1 lb. butter - or oleo - 2 medium onions.
½ lb. Parmesan cheese (grated)
1 cup N.Y. State cheese (grated)
½ tsp. nutmeg - salt to taste -
2 tbsp. Worcestershire sauce
4 tbsp. bacon drippings

Brown round steak in melted butter. Remove steak - add 1 cup water. Grind steak, lemon, onions, peppers and garlic through meat grinder. Add all ground ingredients - also the tomatoes, tomato sauce, Worcestershire sauce, salt, nutmeg, and bacon drippings to the heated gravy and put in a large pot. Bring to a boil - then turn heat on low. Cook 1½ hours. Add cheese. Uncover pot and stir often. Cook until thick. Boil 4 small pkgs of spaghetti. Drain and wash. Place alternate layers of spaghetti and sauce in a casserole. Over top, sprinkle Parmesan cheese. Serve very hot. This serves 20 people.

Mrs. Frank Litchfield

Welsh Rarebit

Melt ¼ lb. butter in large skillet. Into this, cut into small pieces 2 lb. cheese. While cheese is melting, put in ¼ tsp. salt, 4 tbsp. Worcestershire sauce. After cheese is thoroughly melted, pour in 10 well beaten eggs, stirring slowly to keep from cooking too fast. When it begins to thicken, pour in slowly 1 pt. of beer which has been opened long enough to become flat.

Mrs. John Tullis

Enchiladas

1 or 1½ dozen tortillas
1 lb grated American cheese
2 large onions, grated or chopped fine
3 tbsp. Crisco
3 tbsp. White Lily flour
6 tbsp. chili powder
boiling water
salt

Melt Crisco in saucepan. Blend in flour and chili powder. Add boiling water, stirring, to make a medium thick gravy. Season with salt. Cook slowly.

Grease 2 oblong pans lightly. Remove sauce from stove and dip tortillas. Lay in pan, sprinkle latter with grated cheese and a little chopped onion, a dash of salt, and roll up. Place in pan with folded side down. Repeat until pan is full of enchiladas placed close together. Sprinkle cheese and onion lightly over their tops. Pour over the chili sauce up to the top of the enchiladas. Heat 10 minutes in a slow oven.

    Mrs. John E. Plunnek
     Air Corps.

62.

Creamed Eggs and Mushrooms

6 eggs hard boiled (20 min.)
1 can (14 oz.) mushrooms
½ stick butter
1 cup milk
3 tablesp. White Lily flour
½ teasp. salt
Nutmeg or La Rosa sherry wine to taste

Melt butter. Stir in White Lily flour and gradually add hot milk and salt. Cook until thick.

Pour the sauce over the eggs and the chopped mushrooms and heat.

        Mrs. Reeves N. McDonald

- Macaroni Ring -

1 c. boiled macaroni rings
1 c. cream
1 c. bread crumbs
½ c. melted butter
½ tsp. onion juice
3 tsp. chopped parsley
1 c. grated American cheese
3 eggs separated and beaten
Salt and pepper

Mix and bake one hour in ring, set in water.

Fill center with creamed chicken and mushrooms.

   Mrs. Howard Gardner

Noodle Pie

1/4 lb. ground pork
1/4 lb. ground beef
1 medium onion
Small amount of cheese chipped or grated
Half package of noodles
1 can tomato soup

Chop onion and brown in lard. Add meat and cook until fairly done, but not brown. Add cooked noodles to the meat mixture, sprinkling in the cheese (just enough cheese to season). Pour tomato soup over entire mixture, mixing slightly, and bake in moderate oven about 60 or 70 minutes.

   Mrs. G. H. Moore

Creole Eggs

1½ cups thick white sauce
1 No. 2 can tomatoes - 1 large bell pepper
2 medium onions - 2 tbsp. bacon drippings
1 small can green peas - 1 tsp. chili powder
8 hard-boiled eggs - salt - pepper

Cut pepper and onions and cook until tender in bacon drippings - but do not brown. Add tomatoes with juice - and cook slowly about ½ hour. Add peas which have been drained. Cook fifteen minutes - stirring occasionally. Put a layer of sauce in casserole - then a layer of sliced hard boiled eggs and cover with white sauce. Continue doing this until all the ingredients are used, topping the last layer with bread crumbs and bits of butter. Brown in the oven for about 15 minutes. Serves 8.

Mrs. Owen Brewer.

Stuffed Eggs with Tomato Sauce

1 can Tomatoes (#2)   1 onion - chopped
1 Tbsp. Worcestershire Sauce   6 eggs - hard-boiled
1 green pepper - chopped   2 Tbsps. butter

Brown pepper and onion in melted butter. Add tomatoes, Worcestershire sauce, salt and pepper to taste. Cook until thick. Cut eggs in half. Season yolks with mustard, salt, pepper and lemon juice. Refill whites. Then press halves of eggs together and roll in bread crumbs. Pour sauce around eggs. Surround platter with crisp bacon.

Cheese Eggs

8 hard boiled eggs   1½ cups cream sauce
1 cup grated N.Y. State Cheese

Divide eggs with small amount of melted butter, onion juice, vinegar, salt, pepper, and finely chopped pickle and celery. Put eggs in baking dish. Stir cheese into cream sauce and season lightly with red pepper. Pour sauce over eggs and bake in oven until hot enough to serve (about 15 minutes.)

Mrs. John Ward

Pressed Veal

2 lbs. veal without bone
4 hard boiled eggs
1½ cup mayonnaise
1 stalk celery (ground)
2 packages gelatin

Cook veal until done with salt, black and red pepper. Soak gelatin in ¾ cup of water. Pour warm liquor from meat over gelatin. Grind meat and celery and put eggs through masher. Add onion, and lemon juice, salt and pepper to taste. Mix mayonnaise with all ingredients. Put in loaf pan and place in refrigerator until congealed.

Garnish with lettuce and tomatoes. This amount will serve sixteen people.

Mrs Harry Bandy

"Dogs A' La Trailer"

2 lbs. skinless frankfurters
4 tbsp. Wesson oil
3 medium sized onions
2 cans Campbell's tomato soup
3 tbsp. Worcestershire sauce
1 soup can water
Dash tabasco
1 tsp. salt
pepper to taste
2 small pieces garlic

Have Wesson oil very hot in large skillet. Add onions and cook slowly until done. Add other ingredients and allow to simmer over low flame for at least 1 hr. Add frankfurters last 10 min. of cooking. Remove garlic and serve mixture on rice or split English muffins, toasted. Serves six.

Mrs. William O. Senter

Spaghetti Ring

2 tbsp. chopped green pepper
2 tbsp. onion
2 tbsp. butter
1 8 oz. pkg. spaghetti
3 eggs
1 cup tomato soup
1 tsp. Worcester sauce
1 pkg. Kraft American cheese

Cook pepper & onion in butter. Add spaghetti, cooked and drained. Add 3 beaten eggs, tomato soup, Worcester sauce, cheese grated. Bake in buttered ring mold 1 hr. at 325°. Unmold and fill center with peas and shrimp heated in butter.

  Mrs. Chas. A. Johnson
   Birmingham, Ala.

Italian Delight

- ½ lb. spagetti
- ½ lb. ground steak
- 1 cup corn
- 1 can tomato soup
- ½ cup olive oil or butter
- 1 cup parmesan cheese
- 1 can mushrooms
- 1 clove garlic
- 1 small onion
- 1 green pepper
- 1½ tsp. salt
- 1 tsp. worcestershire
- dash paprika
- dash cayenne

Chop onion, add pepper and fry in olive oil until brown. Crush garlic, with salt added, and mix with the above. Melt cheese in heated soup and add spagetti, which has been cooked in salt water, cooked ground steak, corn, mushrooms and seasonings. Stir over fire five minutes. Put in casserole with bread crumbs on top. Bake twenty minutes.

Mrs. Ralph Lawrence
Pittsburgh, Penn.

Chow Mein

1 hen 17 3/4 pounds, or 2 small hens, weighing total 8 pound
1 pound fresh mushrooms.
2 cans bean sprouts
2 cans Chinese vegetables
2 cans Chinese noodles.
5 cups chopped celery.
5 onions
4 tbsp. black molasses.
Thickening
Chicken stock.

Brown onions in skillet. Add mushrooms and cook until done. Boil hen very tender. Cut off meat and mix with onions and mushrooms. Add celery, molasses, vegetables, sprouts, salt and pepper. Cook. Add a little chicken stock and thickening (White Lily flour). Heat noodles in flat pan. Serve chow mein over hot noodles. Serves 22 or more.

Mrs. William Marks S.

American Chop Suey

1 lb. round steak ground with pinch of salt. Brown in 4 tbsp. fat. Cook 1 c. rice and add to meat. Add 2 c. chopped celery, 3 chopped green pepper, 1 pt. tomatoes, small can mushrooms, 2 small onions, and season with salt and pepper. Cook in thrift cooker 20 min. on high and 60 min. on low.

Mrs J. O. Collins
McBean, Ga.

= Creole Brains =

2 sets pig brains — 1 can mushrooms — 1 c. cream sauce — 3 hard boiled eggs 1 c. chopped celery. Cook brains til tender, season with salt and pepper. Butter baking dish. Put a layer of brains, then sliced eggs, celery, and mushroom sauce. Repeat til dish is full. Cover with bread crumbs and brown.

Mrs R. E. Steiner Jr.

Jamaica Curry

2 cups cooked lamb.
4 apples.
4 large Bermuda onions
3 tbsp. cream.
2 tbsp. vinegar
1 tbsp. Worcestershire sauce.
Curry powder to taste.

Put butter into an iron skillet. Fry onions and apples to a golden brown. Reduce heat, add lamb and 1 cup stock or gravy. Add cream, vinegar, Worcestershire sauce and curry powder. Simmer slowly, stirring frequently.
Serve in a ring of rice. Sprinkle fresh grated cocoanut over center.
Serve as condiments
Chutney
Fried onions
Toasted cocoanut
Chopped bacon
Ground peanuts.
Chopped hard boiled egg.
Serves 6

Martha Gardner Calloway
Air Corps.

Cheese Souffle

1 tbsp. White Lily flour   2 tbsp. butter
1 c. sweet milk   3 beaten egg yolks
1½ c. New York State cheese grated
Whites of 4 eggs beaten

Put flour and butter in saucepan, stir until well blended. Add milk, stir until mixture thickens. Cool. Add cheese, salt and yolks to above mixture. Blend well. Stir in slightly beaten whites. Pour into a deep well buttered baking dish and bake in moderate oven 25 minutes.

Mrs. B. A. Taylor

Shrimp Croquettes

1 tbsp. butter   ½ tbsp. White Lily flour
1 c. sweet milk   Salt and pepper to taste

Make a cream sauce of this and cook until thick.

Clean shrimp, cut into halves. Add: cream sauce, Worcestershire sauce, ½ tsp. ketchup. Make into balls. Put into ice box until cold. Roll in cracker crumbs and fry in deep hot fat.
Serve with tartar sauce.

Mrs. Fred Wilkerson

Mushroom Omelet

8 eggs beaten separately   2 c milk
3 tbsp. White Lily Flour   4 tbsp La Rosa sherry
salt and red pepper   3 tbsp. melted butter
1 can mushrooms drained and cut in halves

Put ½ butter in mixture. Pour into greased pan. Put balance of butter on top omelet. Cook 30 minutes in moderate oven.

   Mrs. Charles A. Thigpen Sr.

Rinktum Diddy

2 cans Campbell's Tomato Soup
1 lb. New York State Cheese
1 or 2 eggs
2 tbsp. onion juice

Season to taste with Worcestershire sauce, tabasco sauce, salt and a dash of garlic. Put soup in heavy frying pan or double boiler (do not cover top of boiler). When warm add eggs which have been beaten a little and added with a cup of water. Add cheese (cut in small pieces) and seasoning. Cook until well blended. Serve on crackers or crisp toast. Put on platter and surround with sliced Bermuda onions.

   Mrs. Ed. Burton

POULTRY
AND
GAME

Mildred Nungester

Wild Duck

This is a delicious dish, seldom made in these days unless one has a huntsman in the family — Disjoint the duck as for frying, using only the breast and upper joints. Salt and dredge in White Lily flour, fry in hot lard.

Have a pot of 1 qt. of well flavored soup stock, add a finely chopped onion, parsley, celery, 1 turnip chopped, little grated lemon peel and dash of cloves and tabasco pepper. Also 1 tbsp. White Lily flour and a glass of La Rosa white wine.

Drop the fried duck into this sauce, cover and let simmer —

— Mrs. Chas. Pollard

Chicken Queen

⅛ lb. butter
1 lb. fresh mushrooms
½ cup La Rosa sherry wine
1 large hen
1 bunch of celery (chopped)
1 cup almonds
1 small onion
Salt & pepper to taste

In water to cover, cook hen till meat falls from bones. Cut into 1 inch pieces. Broil sliced mushrooms & onion. Add butter and seasonings (except sherry). Blanch almonds & slice. Thicken chicken stock with White Lily flour. Combine all — add sherry when ready to serve. Pour over tiny, freshly made biscuits, cover with same. In casserole. Serves 6 or 8.

  Mrs. J. W. Mac Queen
   Birmingham, Ala.

Steamed Chicken.

Use 1 hen and ½ lb. veal. Cook until tender. Grind to-gether: 1 bell pepper, celery, salt, pepper, and onion. To 1 cup stock, add 1 tsp. Worcestershire sauce, ½ cup milk, lump butter. While hot, beat into stock, 3 egg yellows. Mix all ingredients and put into pan. Steam for 1 hr.

Sauce

1 large can mushrooms
1 tbsp. corn starch with melted butter
2 tbsp. tomato catsup
Worcestershire sauce to taste

Mrs. John R. Matthews

Chicken Mousse

3 egg yolks
1 1/2 cups milk
1 1/2 tbsp. gelatine
1/4 cup cold water
2 cups minced chicken
1 can mushrooms
1 pt. whipped cream
1/2 cup hot chicken stock
1/2 cup mushroom stock
Salt, pepper, lemon juice.

Mix yolks, milk and cook until custard-like. Soak gelatine in water, then dissolve in hot stock. Stir into custard then add mushrooms and chicken. When cool add whipped cream and mold.

Dressing for Mousse

2 cups mayonnaise
1 cup whipped cream
Juice 1 lemon — 1/2 grated onion
1 cup halved almonds —

Mrs. Carney Laslie

Chicken Croquettes

2 cups chopped chicken
½ tsp. salt.
1 tsp. celery salt.
1 tsp. lemon juice
1 tsp. chopped parsley
Grated rind of 1 lemon
Few drops onion juice
   Mix with 1 cup thick white sauce —
2 tbsp. butter
1 tbsp. White Lily flour.
1 cup milk.
   When cold, mold into shape, dip into beaten egg, roll in bread or cracker crumbs and fry in deep hot fat. Serve with Creole sauce consisting of —
1 can tomatoes
chopped green pepper
1 bay leaf.
Season with tomato catsup, butter, salt, pepper and whole spices. Thicken with White Lily flour.

Mrs. W. D. Moore.

Chicken à la King

4 cup Chicken, Diced   3 Eggs (Hard-boiled)
1 large can mushrooms   2 Tbsp. butter
2 large green peppers   2 cups thin cream
2 cups Chicken Stock   juice 1 lemon
3 Tbsp. White Lily flour   1 cup celery

Salt, black pepper and red pepper to Taste.

Chop mushrooms, peppers and celery. Cook in Stock until Tender. Make a Cream Sauce. Add the mushroom mixture to cream Sauce, Then add chopped eggs, seasonings and last the lemon juice. Let cook in a double boiler until thick.

         Mrs. W. W. Brame

Chicken Tetrazini

Cook 5 lbs. chicken with 1 small onion until very tender. Put in boiler and let simmer 2 or 3 hours: 2 cans tomatoes, strained; 1 grated onion; 2 tbsp. paprika; 1 tbsp. Worcestershire sauce; 1 tbsp. butter. Two hours before serving add chicken, which has been minced, to the mixture, then slowly add 1 pt. cream. About 20 min. before serving add 1 can mushrooms and ½ lb. grated cheese (New York State). When ready to serve add 1 lb. cooked spagetti, or enough to take up the liquid. Sprinkle grated cheese on top.

Mrs. Harold Weatherby

Creme de Volaille

3 cups ground chicken
1 can mushrooms ground
1 cup cream sauce
1 tsp. butter melted
1 tsp. minced parsley
3 eggs
1 tsp. grated onion
1 pkg. unsweetened gelatine

Mix chicken, mushrooms, cream sauce; add butter & eggs, beat hard. Last add parsley, onion & gelatine dissolved in a little water. Season to taste with salt, black & red pepper. Put in a greased mold & steam 1¼ hrs. Unmold & serve with a rich cream sauce with mushrooms.

    Mrs. Dudley Hale
    Air Corps, U. S. A.

Chicken Pie

½ cup Chicken fat, or butter –
¾ cup flour –   2 cups milk –
Pepper to taste –   1½ tsp. salt –
2 cups Chicken Stock and 3 cups of cooked Chicken cut in rather large pieces.

Melt fat (or butter), add flour and mix well. Add milk slowly, then Chicken Stock and seasoning and mix until thick. Add the Chicken and heat thoroughly. Make a biscuit dough and bake biscuit squares in hot oven. Split biscuit squares and arrange the Chicken mixture between and over them.

Mrs. C. L. Coleman

Hot Chicken Ring with Mushroom Sauce

2 tbsp. White Lily flour
2 tbsp. butter
1 wine glass La Rosa sherry
2 cups milk
½ cup stale bread crumbs grated
2 cups chicken meat chopped
2 eggs – beaten separately
Salt and pepper

Melt the butter, add White Lily flour, milk gradually, bread crumbs and cook 2 minutes. Add salt, pepper, chicken meat and allow to cool. Beat egg yolks, add to this mixture and fold in well beaten egg whites.

Grease a ring mold and line with waxed paper. Pour mixture into mold and set in a pan of hot water. Bake in the oven about 35 minutes. When done, unmold on a hot dish and fill center with hot creamed mushrooms. Garnish with parsley and sprinkle a dash of paprika on the chicken.

    Mrs. W. Boyd McGehee

- Creamed Chicken -

1 small hen, chopped — ¾ lb. American cheese
1 bottle small olives
2 cups cream sauce — 1 can mushrooms

Grate cheese & add to chicken. Halve mushrooms; cut olives in small pieces - mix both with chicken. Place mixture in top of double boiler and add rich cream sauce. Heat until cheese has melted. Season to taste and serve on toast or in patty shells.

    Mrs. James Little

Pressed Chicken

1 - 5 or 6 lb hen   1/4 cup cold water
2 carrots   2 stalks celery
1/2 tsp. ground sage 1/2 bay leaf
1 tbsp. gelatin   4 hard boiled eggs

Roast or steam hen with carrots, celery, bay leaf and sage. When very tender, separate meat from bones. Put through food chopper with eggs, using coarse knife. Soak gelatin in cold water 5 minutes. Dissolve in 1 pint of hot chicken stock. Cool until almost ready to jell. Add meat and press down into molds. Attractive designs may be made in the bottom of molds before adding chicken with sliced stuffed olives, green pepper slices, hard egg slices and parsley. Let stand overnight or for 5 or 6 hours. Serve on lettuce with mayonnaise. Garnish with tomatoes, eggs & pickles.

Mrs. C. M. Donnelly.

Creole Chicken

2 hens

Cut chicken in individual pieces, dredge in flour, and brown in hot fat.

Make sauce of 2 garlic buttons, 1 onion, 2 cans tomatoes, 1 teaspoon thyme, 1 teaspoon salt. Cook slowly for 1 hour. Then pour sauce over chicken, adding 1 pound seeded currants, 1 pound blanched almonds. Cook 1 hour in oven in covered pan. Serve poured over rice.

   Mrs. I. B. Feagin
    Birmingham, Ala.

Roasted Quail

Wash quail twice, dissolving a teaspoonful of baking soda in the second water. Rinse. Wipe each bird with a soft linen cloth. Place an oyster in each quail and wrap with soft twine and two slices of bacon secured with toothpicks. Place in roaster, pour a little boiling water over each bird and roast from twenty to twenty-five minutes. When birds are tender, remove bacon, wash with butter, dredge with flour and brown.

Serve on rounds of buttered toast.

Mrs. L. D. Rouse

Turkey Dressing

6 cups toasted biscuit crumbs
2 cups egg bread, crumbled
milk   onion
5 eggs   nutmeg
    Salt and pepper

Toast day-old biscuits and grind. Add crumbled bread. Add broth from boiled liver and gizzard. Add enough milk to make mixture medium soft. Add eggs, chopped onion, nutmeg, and salt and pepper to taste.

Mrs. Fannie L. Oliver

Raw Cranberry Sauce

1 qt cranberries   2 apples
2 large oranges.   2 cups sugar
½ orange peel.

Cut oranges in small sections with scissors. Do not peel but core apples. Run all thru food chopper, using coarse knife. Add sugar and stir well.

           Eva B. Purefoy

Quick Cranberries

1 qt cranberries   1½ cups sugar.
       1¼ cups water.

Place over hot fire, stirring constantly. Boil hard for 10 minutes. Pour in coarse strainer & mash through.

           Mrs. F. H. Edmaro

Cranberry Ice.

2 qts cranberries
4 cups water

Cook until berries are tender. Strain through colander. Add to this:
juice of 8 oranges   4 cups sugar
juice of 8 lemons   1 pint water
Freeze. Makes 1 gallon of ice

           Mrs. Edward Gresham

Apples and Bananas

Peel apples and put layers in pan, then a layer of bananas and so on until pan is full. Add small amount of sugar and 1 Tbsp. of water, if apples are not juicy. Dot with butter and cover with toasted bread crumbs. Cook in a slow oven about 45 minutes.

— Mrs. H. S. Bartlett

Stuffed Peaches

1 can Del-monte peaches
½ lb. dates   1 10¢ bottle cherries
½ cup nuts

Grind ingredients and moisten with cherry juice. Stuff each peach half.

— Mrs. Dan Haygood

MEATS and SAUCES

Creamed Mushroom Sauce

1 pt. cream
1 lb. fresh mushrooms or
    1 large can
lump of butter the size
    of egg
4 tbsp. La Rosa Sherry Wine
2 tbsp. Worcestershire Sauce
salt to taste
1 tbsp. White Lily Flour.

Clean mushrooms, cut in halves if large. Boil 40 min in clear water. Drain and add butter. Let simmer for 15 min. in butter. Drain (save butter) and add cream sauce. To make cream sauce, use double boiler and the same butter and 1 tbsp. flour. Add sherry and seasonings.   Mrs Lister Hill

Pickwick Sauce.

½ pint mayonnaise
½ pint Chili sauce
2 tbsp. Tarragon vinegar
1 tbsp. Anchovy sauce
1 tsp. Tobasco sauce.
    Fred Ridolphi

Dunk your Shrimp

Cream 3 sardines well. Blend in ½ cup mayonnaise, ½ cup Chili sauce, 4 dashes Tobasco, 1 tsp. Worcestershire sauce, ½ tsp. celery seed, 1 pinch of sugar, 1 tsp. Tarragon vinegar, 1 tbsp. capers.

Let stand 24 hours before serving. Serves eight.
    Mrs. Tilghman Turner.

Shrimp Cocktail Sauce

3 tbsp. catsup
1 tbsp. chili sauce
1 tbsp. Worcestershire
½ tsp. salt
½ tsp. mustard

2 tsp. Heinz India Relish
2 tbsp. lemon juice
1 tbsp. mayonnaise
½ tsp. horseradish

Mix all ingredients together and chill well before serving.

Mrs. A. C. Watson

Fish Sauce

Thick cream sauce well seasoned. Boil pieces of fish bone with water (making fish stock). Add yolks of 2 eggs, onion, lemon juice, then add sauce and 3 tbsp. of LaRosa sherry wine after taking off stove. Put mushrooms over fish and sauce. Preferably used with large flounder.

Mrs. D. F. Stakely

Mustard Sauce.

1 medium size box Coleman's mustard.
Add vinegar to make a smooth mixture like heavy cream, sugar and salt to taste. Cook to smooth paste and set aside to cool. Mix with a medium size jar of Kraft Mayonnaise

Mrs. Grood Salter

Tartar Sauce

To 1 cup mayonnaise, add
1 tsp. onion juice
1 tbsp. capers.
1 tbsp. finely chopped sour pickle.

Mrs. John Martin

Sauce For Baked Ham

Stir together:
½ tsp. black pepper — ½ tsp. salt.
1 tsp. dry mustard — 1 tbsp. sugar
½ cup cider vinegar — 1 egg slightly beaten

Put on stove to heat. Then add:
1 cup tomato catsup — ½ cup tart jelly
Let come to a boil, and serve. This sauce is good either hot or cold, and will keep for several days —

    Eleanor F. Graves —

Horse Radish Sauce

½ cup. cream —
3 tbsp. mayonnaise
1 tbsp. cider vinegar
1 tsp. prepared mustard
2 tbsp. bottled horse radish (drained)
½ tsp. salt
Dash cayenne

Whip cream until fairly thick — then fold in mayonnaise. Stir in the vinegar very slowly. Add horse radish, mustard, salt, and cayenne. Chill, and serve with meat.

    Mrs. A. L. Coleman —

Mushroom Sauce

Melt 1 Tbsp. butter.
Stir in 1 Tbsp. White Lily flour.
When light brown, stir in liquor
of 1 can mushrooms. Add 2 Tbsps. catsup,
1 Tbsp. Worcestershire and mushrooms.
Season with salt and pepper. Boil
15 minutes. Then pour over steak.
     Mrs. R. E. Steiner, Jr.

Sauce for Croquettes

1 small can English peas (not drained)
1 small can mushrooms (drained)
1/4 cup cooked celery
1/4 cup cooked green pepper
1/2 large bottle catsup
1 Tbsp. butter
1 Tbsp. White Lily flour
Salt and pepper
Juice and grated rind of 1/4 lemon
Combine ingredients and thicken with
flour, mixed with a little water.
     Mrs. George Robbins

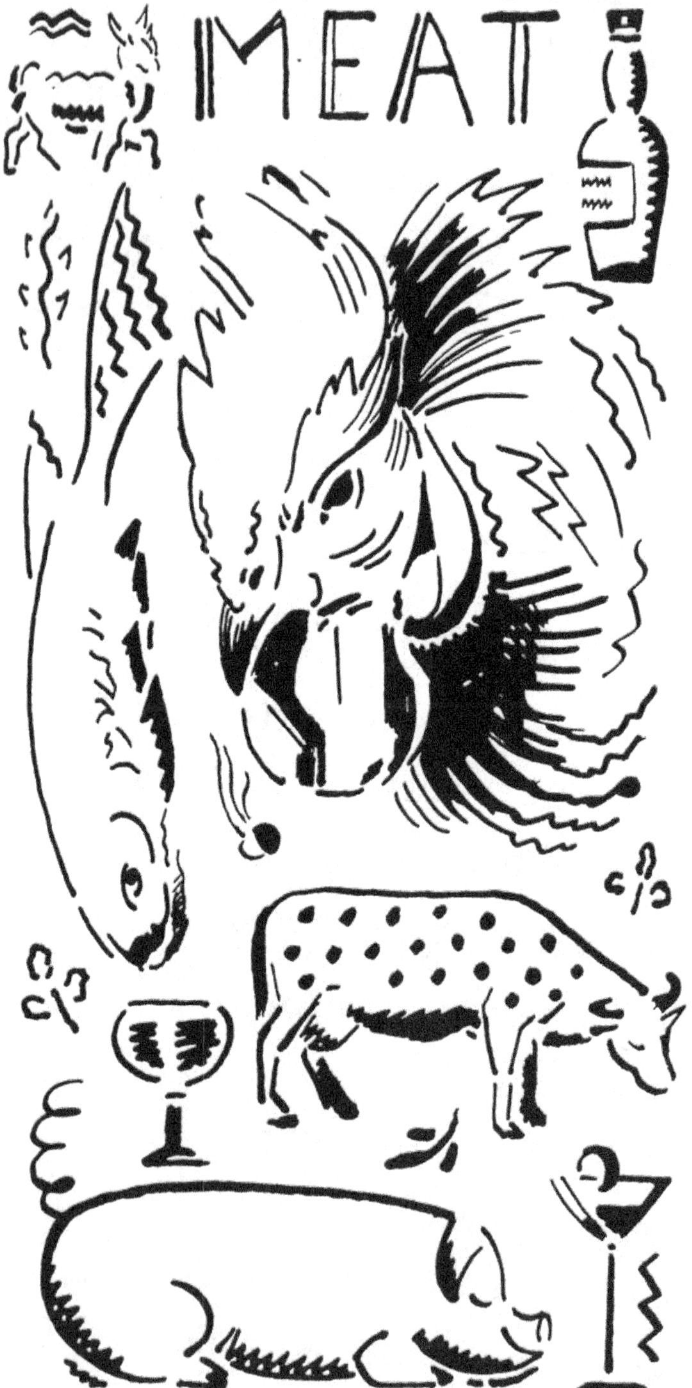
MEAT

Roast Lamb

Wash roast and wipe dry. Rub over 2 tbsp. butter and dredge with White Lily flour sifted with little red pepper. Place in uncovered roaster and brown quickly. Add 1 pt. boiling water, tabasco, 1 onion and 1 carrot sliced. Place 6 strips bacon across top. Cover and bake slowly for thirty minutes and then begin to baste with Barbecue Sauce every fifteen minutes until done.

Barbecue Sauce

3/4 cup vinegar
1/4 cup water
1 tbsp. salt

4 tbsp. butter
6 tbsp. catsup
1 tbsp. Worcestershire
1 cup boiling water
Cayenne and tabasco

Mix first four ingredients and bring to boiling point. Add other ingredients. Baste meat frequently.

Mrs. L. M. Bashinsky
Troy, Ala.

– Veal Birds Stuffed with Wild Rice –

Have butcher cut 3 one-half pound slices of veal round steak and cube. Each piece makes two nice birds.

Stuffing

½ lb. wild rice – 1 stick butter
2 or 3 medium bell peppers – salt
2 or 3 medium onions – pepper
1 tsp. celery seed – dash of tabasco.
2 tbsp. Worcestershire Sauce –

Method of Cooking

Simmer pepper and onions in melted butter until soft but not brown. Add seasonings - then add drained boiled rice. Let get thoroughly cold.

Salt & pepper veal and put a generous ball of rice stuffing on meat & pin up with toothpicks. Dust with flour and fry like country-style chicken - letting the birds simmer in gravy about 1 hr. This makes 6 servings.

    Mrs. Edward Graham -

- Meat Loaf -

2 lbs. beef - 1 lb. pork -
2 cups stale bread crumbs
soaked in 1 cup sweet milk -
1 small onion - few stalks celery -
1 small green pepper - 2 eggs -
Seasonings as desired.

  Have water in pan about half way up the loaf. Baste with small can of Del Monte tomato sauce. Bake for an hour and a half in a moderate oven.

    Mrs. Mason Martin
      Birmingham -

Veal Chops

6 veal chops or cutlets
2 tbsp. lard
2 tbsp. White Lily flour
1/8 tsp. thyme
1 clove garlic
1 lemon
1 bay leaf
1 tsp. Worcestershire sauce
salt and pepper

Have veal chops cut thick. Rub frying pan with a cut clove of garlic, and melt lard in it. Season flour with thyme and cayenne pepper. Dredge chops with seasoned flour and brown in hot lard. Place a slice of lemon on each chop. Add bay leaf, Worcestershire sauce and 1/2 cup hot water. Cover and let cook slowly for 1 hr.

Mrs. L. M. Bashinsky

Boeuf à la Stroganoff

1 lb. cubed steaks or filet of beef
1½ lbs. fresh mushrooms
½ lb. butter
½ pt. sour cream (a tiny bit of vinegar or lemon juice will do)
Salt and pepper to taste

Sauté the mushrooms in butter. Add beef and cook until tender. Add sour cream and cook ten minutes. Serve on buttered Holland Rusk or on rich, toasted big biscuits —

Mrs. D.D. Hale
Air Corps

Spiced Pot Roast with Prunes

4 lbs. round boned roast of beef
1/3 cup vinegar plus 1 2/3 cups water
1/2 lb. prunes
6 cloves
1/8 tsp. ginger
2 cups cooked noodles

Flour the roast and brown on all sides in hot fat. Add salt and spices, cover with water and vinegar and let simmer slowly for 2 1/2 hrs. in covered pot roast kettle. Add washed prunes and cook 1 1/2 hrs. more. Serve meat surrounded with prunes and cooked noodles.

    Mrs. J. Louis Snow

Barbecued Steaks

For out-door grill. Spread individual steaks with soft butter; sprinkle with salt and pepper. Place on grill over hot coals. Have hot sauce on saucepan with back of grill. Use pastry brush to baste steaks with sauce every few minutes. Turn steaks and continue to baste frequently until done.

Sauce

- 1 stick butter
- 1 medium size clove garlic minced
- 1 large bottle tomato catsup
- ½ of 5 oz. bottle Worcestershire Sauce
- 1 10¢ bottle Durkee's dressing
- 2 or 3 very thin slices lemon

Cook butter and garlic together. Add other ingredients and bring to a boil. Drop in the lemon slices and boil for about 2 minutes.

This sauce is excellent to use on roast leg of lamb also. Prepare lamb as usual and cook in oven 3/4 hour, add sauce to gravy and baste frequently until lamb is done. This sauce can also be used to barbecue chickens on an out-door grill.

    Mrs. Micael Microsi

Oven Broiled Steak with Mushrooms

2½ lbs. Porterhouse or tenderloin steak - 1½ inches thick -
¼ lb. extra fat - 1 tsp. lemon juice
½ stick butter - 1 tsp. salt -
1 tbsp. Worcestershire sauce -
¼ tsp. black pepper - ¼ cup water
1 tsp. minced chives or ½ tsp. onion
1 small can chopped mushrooms.

Heat oven to 550°. Mince half of fat and sprinkle over steak. Set broiler two inches below flame and broil steak ten minutes until crisp and brown. On top of stove melt remaining fat, and add all ingredients except butter, mushrooms, and water. Baste steak with half of this sauce and turn. Spread top with fat from pan, and proceed as before. Remove to platter. Pour off excess fat in pan. Add butter, water, and mushrooms. Bring to a stiff boil and pour over steak. Garnish with parsley, and serve thick broiled apple rings as an accompaniment.

Mrs. J. Y. Brame -

Pork Chops Creole.

Flour pork chops. Put in skillet with a little lard and brown. Take out and put in skillet a layer of onions, fresh tomatoes and chopped green peppers, salt and pepper, a dash of cayenne. Add a little water. Put chops back in skillet. Cover and bake 20 minutes.

Mrs. J. G. Hume.

Pork Chops and Sauerkraut

1½ lbs. pork chops
1 large can sauerkraut
2 large tart apples
1 large onion
Salt and pepper.

Wipe chops, sprinkle with salt, pepper, and flour. Place in hot skillet and brown slowly. Chop the apple and onion, mix both thoroughly with sauerkraut. Make brown gravy in skillet where chops were cooked. Add gravy to chops and steam slowly til chops are tender, two or three hours.

Mrs. Cy Brown

Tennessee Stuffed Ham

Boil ham in vinegar, brown sugar, and water until tender. While still warm, stick holes with a cut of a sharpened broom handle. Stuff these holes with the following mixture:

11 hard boiled egg yolks.
lump of butter - size of an egg
1 pt. of Cross & Blackwell pickles
3 cups bread crumbs
2 tbsp. sugar -

Knead with hands to a soft consistency. Spread the remaining dressing over the ham and brown to a light color in the oven. Do not cut until cold. Serve with cooked apples, colored red and green.

   Mrs. Atlee Jordan -

Deviled Ham with Wild Rice

For each portion, spread both sides of baked ham slices with a thick mixture of mustard and bread crumbs. Place in fireproof dish, dot with butter and sprinkle with sugar. Brown 15 minutes under moderate broiler. Steam wild rice and mix with chopped mushrooms fried in butter with minced onion and green pepper.

              Mrs. W. L. Van Pelt.

Veal or Brain Cutlets

Boil 2 sets calf brains for 30 minutes or use 3 lbs. cooked ground veal. Make thick sauce in double boiler of 1½ cups milk, 2 eggs separated and beaten — 2 tbsp flour — 1 tsp salt — 1 tbsp. butter. When sauce is cool add meat and shape into croquettes — roll in bread crumbs and fry in deep fat.

              Mrs. Jack McLemore

Bar-B-Q Ribs

Salt and pepper thick pork ribs. Put the ribs on a sheet of pork on a barbe rack at least 1 foot above charcoal coals. Cook very slowly for 3 hours or more. Turn every 5 minutes and brush or mop meat with the following sauce

4 cups vinegar
1 tbsp prepared mustard
1/4 cup Worcestershire sauce
1/2 cup butter

When meat is thoroughly cooked and well browned, remove from pit. Cut in pieces and serve with the following sauce:

1 large onion browned in 1/4 lb. butter
1/2 cup catsup
1/2 cup chili sauce
1/4 cup Lea & Perrins sauce
1 tbsp Worcestershire sauce
juice of 1 lemon.

Mrs. John Martin.

Steak Martinique

Squeeze lime juice over both sides of the steak an hour or more before cooking. Then prepare a paste made of crushed garlic, freshly ground black pepper, and salt. Smear this paste on both sides of the steak and sear over glowing coals in a charcoal brazier or out-door fireplace. This keeps the meat juices in, after which you can broil the steak to your own taste.

      Camille Brown

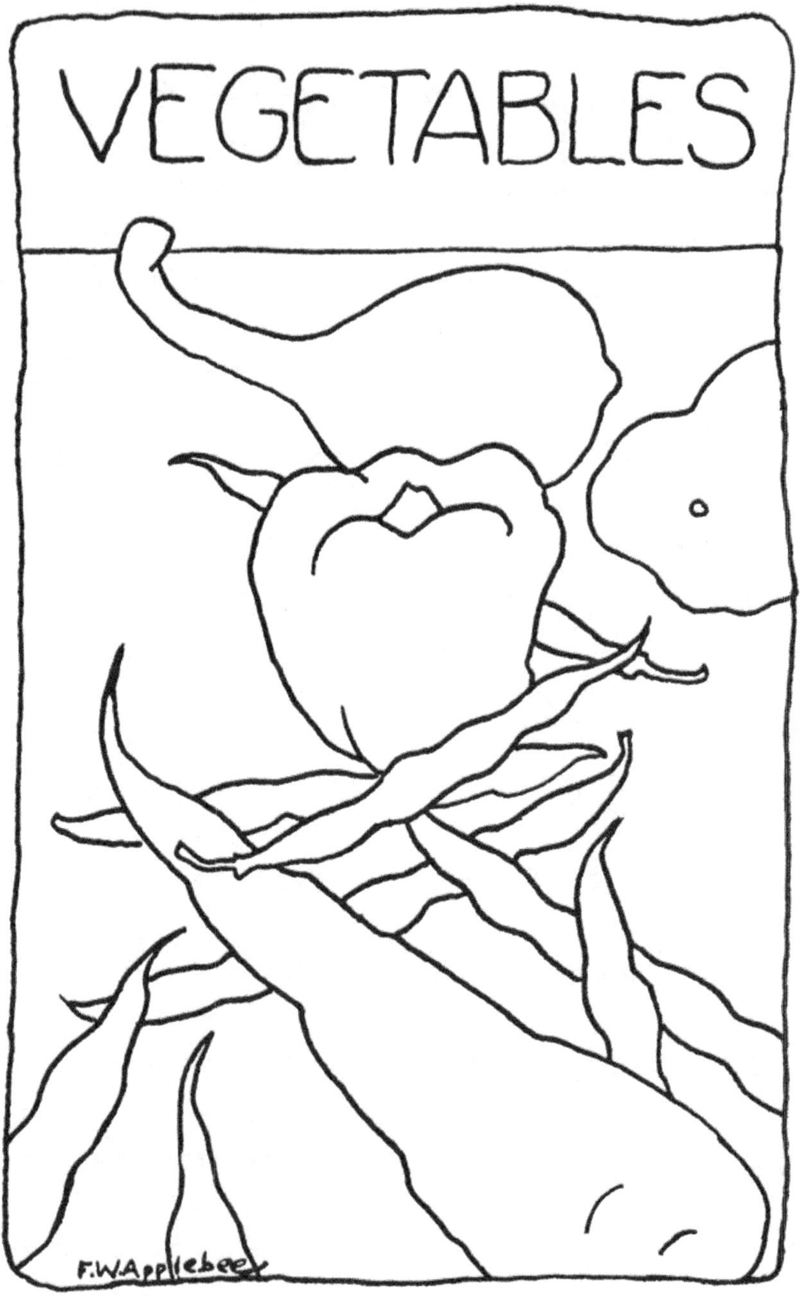
VEGETABLES
F.W.Applebee

Spinach Ring

2 hard boiled eggs - mashed - 2 raw eggs
2 lbs. spinach - 1 cup cracker crumbs
1 hard boiled egg - sliced - 1 stick butter
1½ cups medium cream sauce - salt
pepper

Boil spinach until tender. Chop up fine. Add to cream sauce ½ stick butter. Combine spinach, mashed hard-boiled eggs, raw eggs, cracker crumbs, ½ stick melted butter, seasoning, and cream sauce. Put in greased ring mold and steam in a hot oven for 25 minutes. Unmold and serve hot with mushroom sauce.

Mrs. Moreland Smith

Squash Soufflé

Make a cheese sauce of the following - and let cool -
2 cups milk - 2 tbsp. flour
½ cup bread crumbs - 3 egg yolks
1 cup grated cheese - ½ cup sugar
1 tbsp salt.

To 3 cups of cooked squash add the cheese sauce. Whip 3 egg whites, and fold into the mixture. Cook in a casserole about 25 min. Serves eight.

Mrs. W. T. Neal
Brewton, Ala.

Baked Stuffed Squash

Steam squash 12 minutes, or until tender. Scoop out, turn shells upside down. Put pulp in colander to drain. Put a little salt in each shell, then mix pulp with salt, pepper, butter, Worcestershire and grated cheese. If watery, put in a few bread crumbs. Place mixture in shells and sprinkle with grated cheese. Bake ½ hour with a little water in pan. Rub a little butter on outside of shells.

Mrs. Giles Crenshaw

Onions en Casserole

6 large white onions
1 cup sweet milk
1 tablespoon butter
3 tablespoons White Lily flour, sifted
2 5¢ packages Tom's Toasted Peanuts

Make white sauce of milk, butter and flour. Let cool. Slice and pull apart in rings, six onions. Boil until tender in water salted to taste. When tender drain off water. Butter casserole and alternate layers of onions, sauce, and peanuts until filled. Peanuts last. Bake until set in moderate oven.

Mrs. Thomas H. Edwards

Egg Plant and Shrimp

- 1 medium size egg plant
- 1 can tomatoes
- 1 cup celery
- ½ small onion
- ½ green pepper
- 1 tsp. parsley
- 3 eggs
- ½ lb. shrimp
- Salt, pepper and Worcestershire to taste
- 4 slices of stale bread

Broil onions, parsley and green pepper in butter until brown. Peel and cook egg plant in a little water until tender - then drain. Soak bread in milk until soft. Then add to egg plant. Cook tomatoes and celery with onions, pepper and parsley for a few minutes. Mix with egg plant, shrimp and well-beaten eggs. Place in baking dish and cover with bread crumbs. Cook for 30 minutes. Grated cheese can be put on top, if desired.

Mrs. J. M. Rawlings

— String Beans Excellente —

1 1/2 lbs. String beans
1 medium onion
3 Tbsps. Wesson Oil
1/2 cup Chili Sauce
Salt
Black Pepper

122. Remove strings and snap or cut into 1 inch pieces. Wash and cook in boiling water until tender — usually from 2 to 3 hours. Add salt the last 1/2 hour of cooking.

Sauce —

Place Wesson Oil in stew pan or skillet. Add chopped onion and cook until delicate brown. Add beans which have been drained. Cook for several minutes. Add chili sauce. Cook slowly until thoroughly mixed. Black pepper may be added to suit the individual.

    Mrs. Cyrus B. Brown

Louisiana Red Beans

1 lb. red beans
¼ lb. bacon squares
2 large onions
2 cloves garlic
2 bay leaves
1 tsp. salt
1 tsp. red pepper
few drops Tabasco

Wash beans, then soak overnight. Fry bacon till brown. Wilt onions & garlic chopped in bacon fat. Add bacon, onions, garlic & fat, & seasonings to beans & cook all in same water in which beans were soaked in deep pot. Boil slowly 4 hours or until beans are tender. Stir occasionally last hour to prevent sticking. Serve with rice. Serves 6.

  Mrs. Charles Llenègre
   Birmingham, Ala.

Baked Beans

2 large cans baked beans
3/4 cup brown sugar
1 tbsp. worcestershire sauce
1 medium onion diced fine
1/2 cup tomato ketchup

Mix well and bake in flat baker for 2 hours in slow oven. Strip with thin slices of bacon and bake 30 minutes. Serves 8.

Loraine L. Nunn

Deviled Peas

1 can tomato soup
1 can green peas
1 small can pimento
1 can mushrooms
1 cup celery (diced)
1 green pepper (diced)
1 cup grated New York cheese
1/2 cup chili sauce
1 tbs. worcestershire sauce
1 1/2 cup cream sauce
6 hard boiled eggs

Drain vegetables. Mix all except cream sauce and eggs. Put layer of mixture in casserole - then layer of cream sauce - then layer of sliced eggs. Continue leaving eggs on top. Sprinkle with buttered crumbs and bake for 30 minutes in medium oven.

Mrs. George Pierson

Asparagus au Gratin

1 cup sweet milk
1 Tbsp. butter
3 Tbsps. White Lily flour - sifted
5 eggs
1 cup grated cheese
1 can Asparagus Tips

Make a white sauce of first 3 ingredients, well-beaten egg yolks and cheese. Let cool.

Drain juice from 1 can asparagus Tips. Cut each piece into 3 parts, add sauce and well-beaten whites of eggs. Pour into buttered mold, set in pan of hot water and bake 30 minutes. To serve, turn out on a platter and garnish with parsley.

— Mrs. Thomas H. Edwards —

Fried Onion Rings

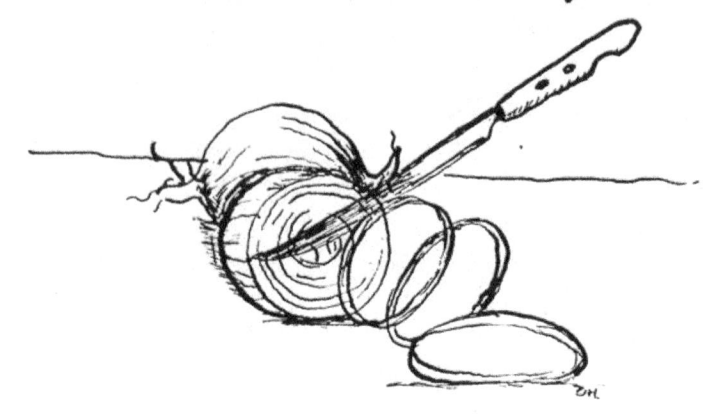

Sliced Onions
½ cup of White Lily Flour
2 egg whites
Salt & pepper
½ cup of corn meal

Soak sliced onions in salt water, then drain. Dip in egg, then in meal. Fry in hot lard. Serve immediately.

   Mrs. Mattie Miller

Potato Puffs

1 cup mashed potatoes
½ cup white lily flour
2 eggs
1 tsp baking powder
Salt, pepper.

Beat yolks until creamy. Add potatoes and mix well. Sift flour, baking powder and seasoning. Add to potatoes. Beat whites stiff and fold into the mixture. Drop from teaspoon into deep, hot fat, and brown.

Mrs. John Danziger.

Fresh Creamed Mushrooms

1 can Heinz Chicken Soup - strained
1 lb. mushrooms
1 Tbsp. White Lily flour
1 cup whipping cream
1 stick butter
salt - pepper.

Pour boiling water over the mushrooms to clean; cut off small pieces of stem. Melt butter in a skillet. Add mushrooms - salt - and pepper. Cover and cook 15 min. or until mushrooms are tender. Add soup & then cream into which flour has been rubbed smooth. Cook 5 minutes more until thickened. Serve on toast.

Mrs. John Danziger -

Asparagus and Mushrooms

1 small can green asparagus
1 small can mushrooms -
2 tbsp. White Lily flour - 1 cup milk
1 tbsp mushroom juice - 1 cup cheese
1 tbsp. asparagus juice - ½ tsp. salt
2 tbsp butter - cayenne pepper.

Cream flour into juices. Melt butter in scalded milk - pour over flour & cook until thick.

Arrange asparagus, cheese, mushrooms, and white sauce in alternate layers. Cover with sauce. Top with bread crumbs toasted a golden brown. Bake.

    Mrs. L. M. Bashinsky -
      Troy, Alabama.

Mushrooms au Gratin

1 lb. mushrooms   1 tbsp. butter
1 tsp. salt   3 tbsp. cream
½ tsp. pepper   3 tbsp. grated onion
¼ cup grated bread crumbs
4 tbsp. grated American cheese.

Wash and peel mushrooms. Arrange mushrooms in a buttered baking dish - sprinkle with salt and pepper. Dot with butter - sprinkle with cheese - bread crumbs - and onion. Alternate layers - finishing with bread crumbs. Dot with butter. Pour in cream and bake in a moderate oven about 25 minutes.

    Mrs. Charles Woodruff.

Corn and Tomato Casserole

4 Tbsp. butter
4 Tbsp. flour
2 cups milk
3/4 teas. salt
Pepper to taste

2 cups cooked corn
4 medium sized potatoes
buttered bread crumbs

1/2 cup grated N.Y. State cheese

Melt butter in double boiler - add flour and mix well. Gradually add milk and cook, stirring constantly until thickened. Add salt and pepper. Place alternate layers of corn, white sauce and sliced tomatoes (sprinkled with salt) in buttered baking dish. Top with bread crumbs and cheese. Bake in 350° oven 'til cheese is melted and mixture thoroughly heated.

   Mrs. W. G. Gilmore

Baked Stuffed Tomatoes

Scoop out pulp of 4 firm, ripe tomatoes. Add pinch of soda and water (if necessary). Simmer until soft. Then add:

1 tsp. salt   Dash of pepper
1 tsp. sugar   1 cup bread crumbs
         1 tsp. baking powder.

Sprinkle tomato cups with salt. Fill with above mixture and sprinkle tops with bread crumbs. Dot tops with butter or strip of bacon. Bake in dry pan until brown (about 15 minutes.)

— Mrs. Roy Cox —

Deviled Egg Plant

Peel egg plant — slice like bread but not through. Place in pyrex dish. Put a slice of onion between each slice of egg plant. Grind a chopped pepper and put over top of egg plant. Pour over this 1 cup French dressing, 1 can tomatoes, 1 cup grated cheese. Place top on dish and bake 3 hrs. Make French dressing of ¼ part vinegar, ¾ parts oil, pepper, 1 tsp. salt and 1 tsp. Worcestershire Sauce.

— Mrs. George Thompson —

Spanish Rice

2 tbsp. fat - 1 cup raw rice
1 small onion minced - 2 tsp. salt
½ green pepper chopped
2 tsp. chili powder - 1 cup tomatoes -
2 cups water

    Wash rice well and dry; brown rice in hot fat. Add onion, green pepper, salt, chili powder, and tomatoes. Mix well and add just enough water to cover the mixture. Cover with lid and allow to simmer until rice is tender (about 30 minutes). Remove lid to allow rice to dry out. Do not stir after cooking starts. Must be cooked very slowly - or the rice will burn.

    Mrs. Aubrey Hornsby -
    Maxwell Field

Mushroom Stuffed Tomatoes 133-

4 firm tomatoes
2 tablespoons butter
2 tablespoons White Lily flour
1 cup milk
1 egg yolk
2/3 cups cooked mushrooms
1 tablespoon chopped celery
1 tablespoon green pepper
1 tablespoon chopped onion
1/4 teaspoon salt
1/8 teaspoon paprika

Wash tomatoes, remove centers, melt butter, add flour. When blended add milk and cook until creamy, stirring constantly. Add other ingredients and stuff tomatoes. Place in shallow pan and add 1/3 inch of water. Bake 30 min. in moderate oven. Will stuff 5 or 6 tomatoes

Mrs. Glenn Andrews

Carrot Soufflé

Make a thick cream sauce using one cup milk, 1 tbsp. butter and 3 tbsp. flour. Add 3 beaten egg yolks, 1½ cup mashed cooked carrots, 1 tsp. salt. Fold in stiffly beaten whites. Turn into greased mold, placing same in pan of water, and cook in 350° oven for about 30 minutes. Fill center of mold with peas or any desired vegetable. Serve hot.

     Mrs. John Blue Hill

Paprika Potatoes

Fry one medium sized onion in butter with one teaspoon of paprika. Add two tomatoes which have been peeled, sliced and drained. Peel two pounds of potatoes, cut in round slices and add. Cover with consommé and cook until liquid has been nearly exhausted. Sprinkle with chopped parsley just before serving.

Mrs. J. H. Elmore

Artichoke and Asparagus

1 can hearts of Artichokes
1 can Asparagus tips
1 cup blanched almonds
1 tbsp. butter
1 tbsp. flour
juice of 1/2 lemon

Make cream sauce with flour, milk, and butter. Add almonds, then drain asparagus and artichokes. Season with lemon juice. Salt and pepper to taste.

Mrs. C. W. Hooper,
Selma, Alabama.

Carrot Ring

2 cups carrot pulp
1 cup milk
3 eggs
1 teaspoon salt
¼ teaspoon pepper
1 teaspoon chopped onion

Cook about 2 bunches of carrots until tender. Press through ricer and measure 2 cups. Season with salt, pepper and onion. Beat eggs slightly, add milk then blend well with carrot mixture. Pour into well greased ring mold and set in pan of warm water. Bake in moderate oven 35 min. Fill center with cooked green peas.

Corn Pudding

1 pint milk
3 eggs, whites & yolks beaten separately
3 tbsp. melted butter
1 heaping tsp. white sugar
1 heaping tsp. cornstarch
1 tsp. salt
6 ears corn

With a sharp knife, slit each row of corn in center; then shave in very thin slices. Add corn to yolks of eggs, butter, cornstarch, sugar & salt. Add milk gradually & last the egg whites beaten stiff. Bake in a hot oven until a light golden brown.

   Mrs. J. P. Galt

Green Peppers with Deviled Cheese Stuffing

1 cup cooked rice
8 medium peppers
1 - 5¾ oz can deviled ham
½ lb. American cheese
3 cups milk
5 tbsp. White Lily flour
3 tbsp. butter
¼ tsp. celery salt
Salt and pepper.

Split peppers lengthwise and parboil 5 minutes. Drain well. Make a white sauce and add rice, ham and 1 cup of cheese to half of sauce. Fill peppers. Sprinkle with cheese and bake in moderate oven 30 minutes. Add the rest of the cheese to remaining white sauce and pour over peppers when served. ½ slice of bacon may be placed on each pepper before baking. Garnish with parsley.

Mrs. Nicholas Robinson

Stuffed Green Peppers

Cut 4 green peppers into halves and clean. Let 3 cups of chopped stale bread soak awhile in milk or water to moisten. Salt and pepper the bread to taste. Add 2 raw eggs, 1 tbsp. butter, 1 1/2 cups chopped shrimp (cooked).

Put this mixture in a double boiler and cook for about 1/2 hour. Take from boiler and stuff the peppers, putting bread crumbs on top of each. Let cook in oven until brown.

Mrs. Hilton Rice

140.

Sweet Potato Balls

Use as many cooked, mashed sweet potatoes as desired (cans of sweet potatoes are easy to prepare). Season, using some red pepper. Add crushed peanuts and 1 or 2 eggs. Form into balls, putting a marshmallow in the center of each. Roll in corn flakes and fry in deep, hot fat. Place on brown paper to drain.

Mrs. W. W. Brown.

For Special Recipes

For Special Recipes

For Special Recipes

For Special Recipes

Salads

Shrimp Ring

2/3 lb. cooked shrimp.
1 cup mayonnaise
1 hard-boiled egg - sliced
1 tbsp. capers -   4 tsp. gelatin -

Soak gelatin in 3/4 cup cold water - then place in pan of hot water until dissolved. When almost cool, stir in mayonnaise. Add other ingredients and juice of 1/2 lemon. Pour in greased ring mold to congeal. Serve on bed of crisp lettuce leaves with bowl of mayonnaise in center.

Mrs. R. S. Hill -

Avocado & Tomato Salad -

1 Tbsp. mayonnaise - 1 tsp. chili powder
1 tbsp. minced onion - 1/2 tsp. salt.
4 avocados -   3 tomatoes
        Lettuce

Mash avocados - add onion, chili powder, & salt. Cut tomatoes in half and fill with mixture. Chill. Serve with French dressing on lettuce. Garnish with a dash of chili powder.

Mrs. Robert Oliver
Maxwell Field, Ala

Asparagus Loaf

Heat 2 Tbsp. butter, 2 heaping Tbsp. White Lily flour. Melt together but do not brown. Pour over 4 eggs, well beaten. Put on fire and stir until thick. Take 1 cup of water from can of asparagus tips. Heat in separate pan. Dissolve 1 envelope of Knox's Gelatin in ½ cup cold water. Stir until dissolved, add to the heated asparagus water, then add to egg mixture. Put on fire and stir until thick. Take from fire, add juice of 2 lemons, season with salt, pepper and paprika. Stir well. Add ½ pint whipping cream—whipped. Cut tips in small pieces, stir into mixture and pour in mold. Serve on lettuce with mayonnaise.

— Mrs. William Titrosi —

Holiday Salad.

2 cups crushed pineapple
1 lemon (juice)
½ cup sugar (scant)
2 tbsp gelatin
1 cup grated cheese
½ pint cream (whipped)
½ cup cold water
2 tbsp pimentoes (chopped)

Soak gelatin in the ½ cup of cold water. Heat pineapple, lemon juice and sugar. Add gelatin. When set, add other ingredients, stirring well. Place in molds until congealed. Serve on lettuce with mayonnaise

Mrs. W. W. Paterson

Pineapple Salad

1 large can grated pineapple
½ c sugar
½ c cold water
2 tbsp. gelatine
½ c lemon juice
¾ c sweet milk
2 Philadelphia cream cheese
1 pt. cream whipped
¼ c mayonnaise

Soak gelatine in cold water; heat pineapple juice, add soaked gelatine and let cool. Mix sweet milk with cream cheese, add other ingredients and place in refrigerator.
Serve on crisp lettuce.

Mrs. Lee Jones

Avocado Salad

2 boxes lemon jello   1 tsp. salt
2 cups boiling water   Dash of pepper
4 Tbsps. lemon juice   1 cup mayonnaise
1 cup whipped cream
2 cups mashed avocado pulp (3 pears)

Dissolve gelatin in boiling water. Add salt and pepper. When cool, add lemon juice. When ready to congeal, fold in mayonnaise, cream and pulp. Turn into wet mold and place in ice-box. Serves 16.

— Mrs. Perry Thomas —

Almond Salad

1 Tbsp. gelatin   1/4 cup sugar
2 Tsps. vinegar   1 Tbsp. lemon juice
1/4 cup cold water   1 cup hot water
1/2 cup each of celery, almonds and stuffed olives, all chopped.
1/8 Tsp. salt

Pour cold water in bowl and sprinkle gelatin on top. Add sugar, salt and hot water. Stir until dissolved. Add vinegar and lemon juice and stir thoroughly. Cool and when mixture begins to stiffen, add remaining ingredients. Pour into mold.

   Mrs. M. H. Pearson —

- Frozen Fruit Salad -
2 large cans cherries
2 large cans pineapple.
2 boxes marshmallows.
2 cups almonds —
1 qt. cream — whipped —
1 qt. mayonnaise
Pack four hours.
  Serves 20 or more —
   Louise Perry Holloway

Corn and Butter Bean Salad

1 cup corn — which has been boiled and cut off
2 cups cooked butter beans
1 green pepper — cut in small pieces
1 cup highly seasoned mayonnaise

Mix all to-gether, season with onion juice, pepper & salt. Garnish with sliced tomatoes and shredded lettuce.

Mrs. Jack Hobbie

Molded Tuna Fish Salad

2 6 oz can tuna fish
2 hard cooked eggs. chopped
½ cup chopped stuffed olives
2 tbsp. capers
1 tbsp. minced onion
1 package plain gelatin
¼ cup cold water
2 cups mayonnaise.

Combine tuna, eggs, olives, capers and onion. Add dissolved gelatin to mayonnaise, stirring constantly. Combine the two mixtures and put in ring mold to chill. When serving, fill center of ring with tomato quarters and avocado slices.

Mrs B. W. Walker
Milstead, Ala.

Appetizer Salad

On a thin slice of bread, which has been well toasted, spread cream cheese which has been flavored with anchovy paste. Place a slice of tomato 1 inch thick on the bread. Top this with ½ deviled egg and over the entire salad pour mayonnaise, which has been seasoned with chili sauce, Worcestershire sauce, and onion juice.

    Mrs. William Lawrence

Black Cherry – Sherry Salad

Stuff 1 can black cherries with blanched almonds. Dissolve 1 package cherry jello in 1 cup cherry juice. Cool and add 1 cup La Rosa sherry wine. Pour into mold.

    Mrs. Albert Smith

Frozen Pear Salad

Freeze a can of Bartlett pears by packing in ice and salt for 5 hours, or in tray of refrigerator. Serve with boiled dressing made of yolks of 3 eggs, 3 rounded Tsp. White Lily flour, ½ cup vinegar, 1 Tsp. dry mustard, ¼ cup cold water, dash red pepper and salt to taste. Cook in double boiler until thick enough to stand. Chill and when thoroughly cold add 1 pt. whipped cream. Add 1 cup pecans, 1 cup raisins and 20 marshmallows, cut in halves. Serves 6.

Mrs. George A. Thomas

Grape Salad

Peel grapes, cut in half and remove the seeds using 1 lb. of grapes and ½ lb. shelled pecans. This serves 8 people.

Dressing

To yolks of 4 eggs, well beaten, add 4 tbsp. sugar, ½ tsp. salt, pinch of cayenne, and 4 tbsp. of vinegar. Put in double boiler and add 1 tsp. butter.

Cook until very thick, stirring constantly. Let cool, and before serving add grapes, nuts, and 1 pt. whipped cream, unsweetened.

Mrs. J. Troy Hails

Frozen Fruit Salad

1 can pineapple - sliced and drained
1 can white cherries - seeded
1 can apricots - sliced
2 cups marshmallows cut in bits
2 cups almonds cut - (optional)

Dressing: whites of 4 eggs beaten stiff
½ cup sugar, pinch of salt
1 Tbsp. White Lily flour
4 Tbsp. vinegar or juice of 3 lemons
Cook in double boiler till thick. When cold, add 1 pint whipped cream. Fold in fruit. Freeze in refrigerator tray 2 or 3 hrs. Serves about 20.

  Mrs. Horace Horner

Stuffed Tomato Salad

8 medium tomatoes
1 lb. American cheese (grated)
5 chopped hard-boiled eggs
6 chopped sweet pickles
3 chopped pimientos
12 chopped stuffed olives
12 chopped pecans
3 tablespoons mayonnaise

Wash, skin, and scoop out the tomatoes. Sprinkle the insides with salt and pepper. Invert on plate and chill. Mix all the other ingredients, and fill tomatoes with it. Serve on lettuce with French dressing.

Mrs. Ben W. Lacy

Bermuda Salad Bowl

1 head cauliflower – separate into flowerettes, slice thin crosswise
½ Bermuda onion sliced into rings
½ cup sliced pimento olives
Marinate in ⅔ cup French dressing 30 mins. Just before serving add one head lettuce broken into small pieces and ½ cup crumbled roquefort cheese. Toss lightly & serve.

       Mrs. Earl Chambless

White Salad

3 egg yolks
2 tbsp. vinegar
½ cup hot water
1 pkg. Knox gelatine
1 tbsp. cold water
1 cup whipped cream
½ cup chopped almonds
1 cup diced pineapple
1 cup white seedless grapes

Soak gelatine in tbsp. cold water to dissolve. Stir eggs in vinegar – add to boiling water, then add gelatine. When cold, add fruit & nuts. Last add cream. Chill in refrigerator. Serve with mayonnaise.

       Mrs. Wylie Hill, Jr.

Congealed Cream Cheese Salad

Cream 2 pkgs. cream cheese (or 1 jar of cottage cheese) with 2 tbsp. of vinegar. Add -

2 chopped pimentos	½ tsp. salt
½ cup olives	½ pt. whipped cream
½ cup sweet pickles	
½ cup nuts	½ cup sugar

Dissolve 1 envelope Knox's gelatine in 1 scant cup of boiling water. When cool, add to the above and pour into molds. To double the recipe use 3 jars cottage cheese, 1 cup of sugar, 2 envelopes gelatine, 2 cups boiling water. When this is congealed between layers of tomato aspic, it makes an attractive salad.

Leila Buchanan

Cheese Salad

1 lb. American cheese	3 pieces of sweet pickle
1 cup pecan meats	
3 pimentos	a pinch of salt
3 hard boiled eggs	

Run through meat grinder. Work like dough. Place in a mold and chill for 24 hours. Slice and serve with mayonnaise on a lettuce leaf.

Mrs. W.W. Yarbrough.

Cucumber Aspic

Soak 2 tbsp. gelatine (Knox) in ½ c. cold water. Dissolve in 2 c. boiling water. Add ¾ c. sugar and stir. Then add ½ c. lemon juice. Add 1 tsp. salt and 1 tsp. green coloring and the juice of 3 or 4 large cucumbers. Mold in ring. To serve fill center with crabmeat or chicken salad.

Mrs Frank Sale
Washington, N. C.

Tomato Aspic With Chicken

Soak 2 envelopes gelatine in ½ c. cold water. Use 3½ c. tomato juice — 2 tbsp. onion juice, 1 bay leaf, salt and pepper to taste. Boil a few minutes and add gelatine while hot. Add 2 tbsp vinegar and strain into individual molds into which diced chicken has been placed.

Mrs J. D. Flowers

162.

Congealed Crabmeat Salad

1 lb. fresh white crabmeat
4 Tbsp. chopped celery
2 cups tomato juice
1/4 cup vinegar
2 packages gelatin
2 Tbsp. sugar
1 Tsp. salt
Juice of 6 lemons
1 Tbsp. Lea and Perrins Sauce

Mix all ingredients, except crabmeat and celery. To this add gelatin, previously dissolved in cold water. Put a layer of crabmeat in mold, cover this with a layer of celery, then add another layer of crabmeat. Pour the other mixture over this and place in ice box to congeal. Serve with Thousand Island dressing. Serves 10 people.

Mrs. John Blue

Potato Salad Special

6 medium potatoes
1 medium onion chopped
1 cup chopped celery
½ cup chopped green pepper
½ cup grated carrot
Juice 1 lemon
1 tsp. prepared mustard
Salad dressing to suit –

Combine all ingredients. A cup of chopped cucumbers and 2 tbsp. chopped pimentoes may be added.

Serve on crisp lettuce and garnish with paprika.

Evelyn Bailey

164.
Caviar Dressing

1 Can Caviar - 2 inches high -
4 hard boiled Eggs - chopped fine -
4 Tbsps. Chili Sauce -   juice ½ lemon -
½ Tsp. Salt -   ¼ Tsp. Pepper -
       4 Tbsps. olive oil -

Mix Chili Sauce, olive oil, lemon juice, salt and pepper and beat together thoroughly. Then add Eggs and Caviar. Serve on vegetable Salad. Serves 14.

Mrs. F. P. Pointer -

Russian Dressing

1 cup stiff mayonnaise
2 tsp. minced green bell pepper
3 tbsp. Chili sauce
2 tbsp. lemon juice
1 tsp. Worcestershire sauce
½ tsp. onion juice

Mix lemon juice, Chili sauce, and Worcestershire sauce together. Stir into mayonnaise and add other ingredients. Chill before using.

Evelyn Mathews

Thousand Island Dressing

Mix together 1 pt. of mayonnaise, 1 large bottle Chili sauce, 1 large bunch of celery, 1 small bottle olives, 2 hard-boiled eggs, and 1 bell pepper. Use on head of shredded lettuce. This is also good over Holland Rusk spread with cream cheese and anchovy, with tomatoes and avocado pears.

Mrs. Fannie S. Oliver

French Dressing

1 can Campbell's Tomato Soup.
1 tsp. Worcestershire Sauce.
1 Tsp. grated onion or juice.
3/4 cup vinegar
2 tsp. paprika – 1 tsp. salt
1 dash Tabasco – 1 cup Wesson Oil.

Put all ingredients except oil and vinegar in a jar. Use egg beater. Add oil – a small quantity at a time – beat well. Last – add vinegar or lemon juice. Makes nearly a quart and keeps indefinitely.

Mrs. J. B. Stratford.

Fruit Salad Dressing

2 whole eggs - beaten lightly
2 tbsp sugar -   2 tbsp. water
2 tbsp. lemon juice - 1 tbsp. butter
½ pt. whipped cream -

Boil mixture of eggs, sugar, water, and lemon juice in a double boiler until thick, stirring constantly. Remove from fire, add butter; cool, and stir in whipped cream.

Mrs. W. C. Bowman -

- French Dressing -

1 small can Del Monte tomato sauce
1½ cups Wesson oil.
½ cup Tarragon vinegar
1 tbsp. Worcestershire sauce
1 tsp. prepared mustard
2 tbsp. white Karo syrup.
1 tsp. - or more - salt -
1 small button of garlic (cut up)
Small amount of grated onion
   and tabasco -

Put all in a container and mix well. Just before serving, crumble Roquefort cheese in the amount to be served.

Mrs. Perry Thomas -

SOUTHERN BREADS

KElly Fitzpatrick.

Beaten Biscuits

BRIDE BLITZ BISCUITS!

2 quarts white Lily flour.
1 tablespoon sugar.
1 teaspoon salt.
1 pinch soda.
1 pinch baking powder.
1 full cup lard.
1 cup ice cold sweet milk.

Sift soda, salt, baking powder into flour. Work lard in well. Add milk. Make this into a stiff dough and work into its beating machine until dough pops like a pistol. Put into biscuits and bake in very slow oven.

Mrs. Fred Wilkerson.

Old-fashioned Buckwheat Cakes

1 cup dark buckwheat flour
1 large Tablespoon White Lily flour

Make a stiff batter with warm water, to which has been added ½ cake yeast. Let rise overnight. In the morning, add ½ Tbsp. syrup, pinch of salt, pinch baking powder and ½ Tsp. soda. Thin with sweet milk and cook on hot griddle.

Mrs. C. B. Hume

White House Recipe for Batter Cakes
(used in Pres. John Tyler's time)

1 cup meal
2 cups water
3/4 tablesp. salt
2 cups White Lily flour
2 tablesp. baking powder
2 tablesp. butter
1 1/2 cups milk
3 eggs

Prepare thick mush by cooking until well done the meal, water and salt.

When done, add butter and stir well. Sift in the White Lily flour and baking powder, then the milk and well beaten egg yolks. Last, fold in the stiff egg whites.

Fry on hot skillet.

Mrs. Charles Marks

Plantation Spoon Bread

2 cups cooked medium ground grits
1 tablespoon butter, melted
3 eggs, separated
1 scant cup sifted meal
1 teaspoon salt
2 teaspoons Baking powder
sweet milk

Mix in order given. Have grits hot. Add milk to make consistency of thick boiled custard. Bake one hr. in medium oven.

Mittie Holt Nicrosi

Spoon Bread

2 cups sweet milk —
1 cup corn meal, sifted —
Put this into double boiler and cook until thick, stirring constantly.
4 eggs - beat well —
1 Tsp. salt —
2 Tbsps. lard or butter —

Add beaten eggs, salt and shortening to thickened meal and milk, pour into hot greased Pyrex dish and bake at 400 degrees for 30 minutes.

— Mrs. Hilton Rice —

Refrigerator Rolls

3/4 cup milk   1 cake yeast
1/4 cup sugar   1/4 cup warm water
3 tbsp. shortening   1 egg
1 tsp salt
3 1/2 cups White Lily Flour

Scald milk, pour over sugar, salt & shortening in mixing bowl. Cool to lukewarm. Add beaten egg. Soften yeast in lukewarm water. Stir into milk mixture. Measure 3 1/2 cups flour & then sift. Add one half of flour to above mixture & mix well. Add rest of flour. Cover bowl with wax paper & towel, place in refrigerator for at least 12 hrs. Two & one half hrs. before baking, take from refrigerator, make into rolls & let rise. Bake 20 mins. in 375° oven. Makes 36 small rolls.

        Mrs. Dunbar Adams

Ginger Muffins

1 cup butter or Crisco - 1 cup syrup -
1½ cups White Lily flour - measured before sifted
3 eggs - 1 tsp. baking powder -
1 heaping tbsp. ginger - dash of cinnamon, allspice, and cloves - pinch of salt sifted with flour.

Cream butter; add flour, syrup, and well-beaten eggs. Bake slowly in well-greased muffin pan. Makes 3 dozen.

Mrs. C. G. Hume -

Whole Wheat Nut Bread

2 cups graham flour
1½ cups White Lily flour
1 tsp. salt - 1 tsp. soda (small)
1 heaping tsp. baking powder
1 cup sugar - ¾ cup pecans
2 cups sweet milk

Mix dry ingredients; then add milk, nuts, raisins, etc. Bake in a bread pan in a moderate oven.

Mrs. N. V. Carson -

Alice Ioea Ledbetter

Illinois Coffee Cake

½ cup sugar
1½ cups White Lily flour
2 Tsps. baking powder
½ Tsp. cinnamon

Mix and sift above. Add 1 egg, 2 Tbsps. melted butter and ½ cup milk or water. Mix and pour into greased pie tin or square cake pan. Sprinkle sugar and cinnamon over top. Bake in moderate oven 35 minutes. Serves six.

Mrs. Gene B. Simmons

Cheese Spoon Bread

1 cup boiling water
1 cup corn meal
1½ teasp. salt
1½ teasp. melted butter
1 cup grated cheese
2 eggs
1½ cups milk
2 teasp. baking powder

Pour water over meal and add other ingredients. Cool and add well beaten eggs, milk and baking powder. Bake in 350° oven for 30 or 40 minutes.

     Mrs. Bernard Steiner

Banana Bread

Mash 4 large, ripe bananas, add 2 eggs. Add 1 cup butter creamed with 1 cup sugar. Then add 4 cups White Lily flour, 1 cup nuts, 1 teasp. soda dissolved in 3 tablesp. cold water, pinch salt. Bake in a moderate oven. A baking powder can is excellent to bake in.

     Miss Caroline Carmichael

Nut Bread

3 level cups White Lily flour
1 cup sugar
6 teaspoons Rumford baking powder
1 teaspoon salt
1 cup nut meats (chopped)
1 egg beaten light
1 cup sweet milk

Sift dry ingredients twice. Add nuts, then beaten egg mixed with milk. Mix to dough. Turn into well greased loaf pan, let stand 15 mins. Bake 45 mins. in a moderately hot oven.

   Mrs. Eugene Carter

Boston Brown Bread

3 cups Graham flour (unsifted)
1 cup corn meal   1 level teas. salt
1 cup syrup   3 level teas. soda in syrup
1 cup buttermilk   ½ package raisins

Mix, fill baking powder cans ¾ full. Place in pan of warm water deep enough to reach half way up cans. Steam 3 hrs. Makes 6 loaves.

   Mrs. D. W. Crosland Sr.

Orange Bread

1 yeast cake
1 tall can condensed milk
1 tall can hot water
2 teaspoons salt
1/3 cup shortening
1 scant cup sugar
Enough White Lily flour to make a thick sponge.
Orange peel

Cut orange rind of ten to 12 oranges in small pieces and soak over night in water salted to taste. In the a.m. boil in 3 waters. Add cup sugar, cook 'til dry.

Dissolve yeast cake in milk and hot water. Add salt, shortening and when shortening is melted, add flour. Let first sponge rise and then cut down and knead in orange peel. Let rise again, then knead lightly and form into loaves. Let rise well in greased loaf pans and bake 45 minutes in a 375 degree oven. Makes about four large loaves.

Mrs. Wm. J. DeWitt

Oatmeal Bread

2 cups boiling water - 1 tbsp butter
½ cup molasses - 1 cup rolled oats
2 tsp. salt - 5 cups White Lily Flour
1 yeast cake - dissolved in ½ cup of lukewarm water

Add boiling water to oats and let stand one hour; add molasses, salt, butter, dissolved yeast cake, and White Lily Flour. Beat thoroughly; let rise; and beat again. Turn into buttered bread pans. Let rise again and bake 40 to 60 min. in a hot oven.

Mrs. Dan Huer.

Date Bread

1 cup dates chopped. Sprinkle with 1 tsp. soda, and pour over this 1 cup boiling water. Let stand until dates soften. Add 1 tbsp. butter - 1 cup sugar - 1 egg - salt - vanilla - and 1¼ cups White Lily Flour. Bake 45 min. in a slow oven.

Mrs. Oscar Covington

Cinnamon Toast.

1 loaf unsliced day-old bread. Cut crust off all four sides. Slice in 3 slices lengthwise. Then in 1 inch strips across. Have ready 1/4 pound melted butter. Brush strips all over. Dip in a dish containing 1/2 cup confectioners sugar, 1/2 cup brown sugar, 1 teaspoon cinnamon well mixed. Be sure strips are thoroughly covered. Bake in a hot oven 5 to 8 minutes. Serve hot.

Mrs. S. R. Damon.

Popovers.

4 eggs
1 1/2 cups White Lily flour
1 cup sweet milk
1/2 cup water
1 rounded teaspoon of butter
Pinch of salt.

Beat eggs together lightly. Then add flour. Add water and milk gradually. Have pans well greased. Bake in moderate oven. Serve immediately.

Mrs. Ernest Marbury

Delsey's Pone Corn Bread

2 c sifted meal
1 tsp. salt
¼ c water
1 heaping tbsp. lard or lard the size of a large egg.
¼ tsp soda
¾ c buttermilk

Cream lard and dry ingredients together using a tablespoon and mixing thoroughly, add slowly the cup of liquid being careful not to make the batter too soft. Mold with hands into 5 or 6 small pones. Put into warm skillet and bake in a moderate oven. Takes about ½ to ¾ hour to bake.

Mrs. William Jordan

Sally Lunn Muffins

2½ cups of White Lily flour
1 cup sweet milk (lukewarm)
2½ tablespoons melted butter
2 tablespoons sugar
½ teaspoon salt
½ yeast cake
2 eggs

    Beat the yellow of eggs until very light. Add the sugar and beat again. Dissolve ½ yeast cake in lukewarm milk and mix with eggs and sugar; add the butter and salt. Sift in the White Lily flour. Then add the stiffly beaten whites. Let rise for about 4 hrs. When well risen beat down the mixture and pour into well greased muffin tins. Let rise for 1½ or 2 hrs. Bake 45 min. in moderate oven. Serve immediately.

                    Mrs. Charles Pollard

Corn Cakes

1 cup corn meal. Sift with a little salt in meal. Break 1 egg into bowl with meal. Stir 1 cup of buttermilk into the mixture & add ¼ tsp. soda. Mix well. If this does not make a thin batter, add a little cold water. Add 3 tbsp of melted bacon drippings — beat, & mix in 1 tsp. baking powder.

          Mrs. John Matthews

Flour Muffins

2 cups White Lily flour   1 cup sweet milk
4 tbsp. Wesson Oil   1 level tsp. salt
2 tbsp. sugar (rounded)   1 egg
1 heaping tsp. baking powder

Mix flour, oil, sugar, salt & milk together. Add well beaten egg & just before baking, add baking powder. Cook in greased muffin rings in a hot oven.

          Miss Evelyn Mathews

Waffles for Electric Irons

2 c. White Lily Flour
2 eggs, separated
1 tsp sugar — 1 tsp salt
2 c. sweet milk — ½ c. melted butter — 3 level tsp. baking powder.

Sift together sugar, flour and salt. Add egg yolks to milk, then add to dry mixture. Next add melted butter and baking powder. Fold in beaten egg whites. Have irons very hot.

Mrs Clifford Lanier

= Buttermilk Waffles =

2 c. buttermilk — 1 tsp soda dissolved in milk — 2 c. White Lily flour — 1 tbsp. corn meal — 1 tbsp melted butter or lard — 1 tsp. sugar
1 large or 2 small eggs. Mix dry ingredients, mix liquid ingredients. Mix together.

Mrs C. G. Hume

DESSERTS.

ICE BOX CAKE

1 large Jane Parker Angel Food Cake
½ pt. cream (whipped)
6 Almond Hershey bars

Melt Hershey bars over hot water. Add very slowly to whipped cream. Ice cake. Chill for at least 12 hours before serving.

        Mrs. Rob't. F. Henry

Parson Jiffy Pudding

Bought sponge cake or lady fingers may be used. Sprinkle blanched almonds over cake and then soak in LaRosa sherry wine about two hours (not too moist.) Pour cold boiled custard over and top with whipped cream.

        Mrs. John R. Danziger

Ice Box Cake

2 doz. day old almond macaroons
1½ doz. fresh lady fingers
1½ cups pulverized sugar
½ lb. almonds or pecans
4 eggs   ½ lb. Butter
½ pt. cream (whipped)
1 small bottle cherries.

Cream Butter and sugar. Beat eggs separately. Add whipped yolks to butter and sugar, then add beaten whites, ground nuts. Split lady fingers, cut off ends and stand around the inside of spring form pan. Put layer of macaroons on bottom of pan and ends of lady fingers. Then a layer of above mixture, then layer of macaroons and so on.

Set in ice box for twenty four hours. Top with whipped cream and cherries. Remove side of pan — slip pan on plate to serve.   Mrs. S. Roemer

Apricot Ice Box Pudding

1 lb. XXXX sugar – 1 cup butter
4 eggs, juice of 1 orange and
1 lemon – 2½# can apricots
1 lb. marshmallows – 2 doz.
lady fingers.

Line spring mold with lady fingers. Pour apricots and juice over them. Add marshmallows, cut in half. Cream butter and sugar, add beaten eggs, and orange and lemon juice. Pour in mold and chill 48 hours.

Mrs. Emmett Poundstone

Coffee Mousse

Add 1 cup sugar to 1 pt. whipped cream. Add 1 tbsp. gelatine, dissolved in ½ cup hot water. Add 1 cup coffee and mold in ice box for forty-eight hours.

Mrs. Frank Scott

Pineapple Icebox Dessert

30 vanilla wafers
1/2 cup sugar
3 tbsp. lemon juice
4 eggs
1 small can crushed pineapple (drained)

Crush wafers — put 1/2 in bottom of loaf pan lined with waxed paper. Boil juice, yolks, sugar and pineapple until thick (stir).

Dissolve 1 tbsp. gelatin in 1/3 cup warm water — add to other mixture — let cool. Beat egg whites adding 1/2 c sugar. Fold into mixture, pour over wafers, cover top with remaining wafers. Chill over night. Serve sliced, and top with whipped cream.

Mrs. J. F. Blue
Union Springs, Ala.

Chocolate Soufflé

2 oz. chocolate, grated fine
6 tbsp. White Lily Flour
4 tbsp. sugar
2 tbsp. butter
1 c. sweet milk
2 egg yolks
3 egg whites - beaten
½ tsp. vanilla

Combine chocolate and milk, simmer until dissolved. Melt butter, stir in flour and add to chocolate mixture. Boil well. Cool a little and add vanilla, sugar, yolks of eggs, (one at a time). Beat well and fold in egg whites. Turn into greased mold and steam 45 to 60 minutes. Serve immediately with plain cream.

Mrs. Erie Catmur

Lemon Pudding

(Simple, inexpensive dessert for winter)

Melt 1 tbsp. butter and add 1 cup sugar and a pinch of salt. Next add juice of 1 lemon and grated rind of 2 lemons. Then add 2 well-beaten egg yolks, 1 cup milk and 2 level Tbsps. White Lily flour. Last add the well-beaten whites of the 2 eggs and bake pudding in a dish (set in a pan of hot water) until pudding leaves side of dish.

This is very good served cold with whipped cream.

Mrs. B. J. Baldwin

Fritters

3 eggs - 1 tsp. soda - pinch of salt
3 tumblersful sifted White Lily flour
2 tumblerful buttermilk

Beat eggs separately. To the yolks, add alternately the sifted flour and milk. Stir in soda. Whisk the whites to a stiff froth and stir into the batter last. Drop into hot boiling lard, and cook a light brown. Drain on brown paper. Serve as a dessert with molasses.

Mrs. C. G. Hume.

Macaroon Pie

9 Premium Soda crackers rolled fine with 1 tsp. baking powder added. Beat whites of 3 eggs until stiff and add 1 cup sugar. Beat well and add 1 Tsp. almond extract, 1 cup chopped pecans. In a pie plate place a generous lump of melted butter. Mix crackers with egg mixture, and put in the pie plate. Bake 20 or 25 minutes at 325°. Serve with whipped cream.

Mrs. M. C. Nation

194.
Congealed Macaroon Pudding

4 eggs   2 tbsp. gelatine
18 macaroons   3/4 c sugar
2½ c milk   pinch salt
3 tbsp. La Rosa sherry wine

Soak gelatine in milk thirty minutes. Place over a slow fire, stirring until milk is hot and gelatine is dissolved. Beat egg yolks and sugar until light and spongey. Add salt. Stir gelatine mixture into egg mixture.

Let cool in ice box until it starts to congeal. Add La Rosa sherry and fold in stiffly beaten whites. Turn into a melon mold lined with macaroons. Garnish with whipped cream and cherries.

Mrs. Chas. Levy

Macaroon Pudding

6 egg yolks
1 tbsp. White Lily flour
1/2 lb. ground almonds
1 cup sugar
1 cup La Rosa sherry wine
2 dozen macaroons

To well beaten egg yolks, add flour, sugar and La Rosa sherry. Beat well. Place in double boiler and stir constantly until thick. Line baking dish with macaroons and cover with sauce. Make meringue of egg whites and 6 tbsp. sugar and sprinkle almonds on top. Place in oven and brown.

Mrs. J. M. Jenkins

Sherry Gelatine

Mix 3/4 c sugar with 3/4 c water and boil 5 min. Soak 1 envelope gelatine in cold water, then dissolve in the warm syrup. When cool, add 1 1/2 c La Rosa sherry wine. Serve with whipped cream. This will serve six people.

Mrs. Pearce N. McDonald

196.

~ Date Pudding ~

2 eggs with 3/4 cup sugar
2 1/2 Tbsps. White Lily flour
1 level Tsp. baking powder
1 cup nuts   1 cup dates, cut fine
Sprinkle with cinnamon and bake in a flat pan. Cut in squares and serve with whipped cream.

    Mrs. A. D. Hargen ~

~ Sweet Potato Pudding ~

Grate 2 medium size raw sweet potatoes. Add 3 well beaten eggs, 1 cup sweet milk, 1 cup sugar, 2 Tbsps. cane syrup, level Tsp. salt, melted butter the size of an egg, dash of nut-meg and cinnamon. Mix well and bake until firm and light brown. Serve with any pudding sauce.

    Mrs. M. C. Nation ~

Caramel Charlotte

Dissolve 1 envelope Knox gelatine in ½ cup cold water. Put 1½ cups sugar in a skillet to melt. Then add to it ¾ cup boiling water - very slowly and stirring constantly. Pour this on to the gelatine - adding 2 tsp. vanilla. Let this cool but not congeal. Add 1 pt. whipped cream and ½ lb. of blanched, chopped almonds. Line a bowl - bottom and sides - with Lady fingers; pour in mixture and put on ice to congeal. Serve with whipped cream.

Leila Dowe -

- Charlotte -

1 qt. whipping cream - ½ cup sugar
3 egg whites - 1 cup sweet milk
2 envelopes Knox gelatine - vanilla to taste
Whip cream and add stiffly beaten egg whites. Dissolve gelatine in ½ cup cold water. Heat milk and sugar to the boiling point - add gelatine and stir until dissolved. Cool by placing in pan of cold water or over ice until mixture begins to thicken. Add cream - egg whites & vanilla. Pour into mold & place in refrigerator to congeal.

Mrs. John Curry -

Boiled Custard

½ pt. whipping cream - 1 cup sugar
½ pt milk - ½ tsp. vanilla
3 eggs (whole) - 2 egg whites

Put cream and milk in top of double boiler and heat. Mix eggs and sugar together - add milk gradually, stirring constantly. Cook until custard thickens. When cool, add vanilla. Place in a pyrex dish - top with meringue made of 2 egg whites and 1½ tbsp. sugar and brown lightly. Coconut may be sprinkled on top of meringue before browning - or added to the custard.

          Mrs. Berney Jones -

Sylabub

1 qt. cream - 1 pt. milk

Sweeten and add La Rosa cherry to taste. Churn in sylabub churn. As foam rises, skim it off and put in glasses. Continue until it is all used. To make it extra thick, churn twice.

          Mrs. W. H. Hubbard -

Spice Cake

½ cup shortening
1 cup syrup
1 cup boiling water
½ cup sugar
1 egg
2½ cups White Lily Flour
1½ tsp. soda (level)
1 tsp. nutmeg, cinnamon and allspice
1 tsp. vanilla

Dissolve soda in boiling water. Cream shortening and sugar. Add syrup, flour and water. Bake in moderate oven. Serve with egg-nog sauce.

Egg Nog Sauce

Cream yolks of 2 eggs with 1 cup of sugar. Add whites beaten stiff. Add 1 cup whipped cream and 2 tablespoons whiskey or ½ cup La Rosa wine.

Mrs. James M. Scott
Scotia, Ala

Bakeless Fruit Cake

½ lb. graham crackers rolled fine
½ lb. marshmallows cut fine
½ lb. dates cut fine
1 cup nuts cut fine
2 small bottles Maraschino cherries
1 pt. whipping cream

Mix fruit, marshmallows, crackers and nuts with cherry juice (add a little thin cream or La Rosa wine if not moist enough)

Press firmly into a tube pan or ring mold lined with heavy wax paper which has been oiled or buttered. Let stand overnight in the refrigerator. Turn out and serve with whipped cream —

Mrs. Ruby Harris
Panama City, Fla.

Lemon Cake

10 eggs, separate, add 1 tbs. of sugar to each egg yolk, beat light, add juice of 4 lemons, rind of 2 grated, 1/2 tbs. of water to each egg; cook until thick. When cool add scant tsp. of baking powder - last fold in beaten whites of 5 eggs. Line spring mold with 2 doz. lady fingers, split, pour in lemon filling. Make meringue of remaining whites (5) Spread on top and bake delicate brown. Serve cold with whipped cream as garnish.

Mrs. R. S. Hill

Date Cake

2 whole eggs   1/2 cup sugar
1 package pitted dates   1 cup nuts
1/2 cup White Lily Flour
1 tsp. vanilla   1 tsp. baking powder

Beat eggs together and add sugar, chopped dates and nuts. Mix with sifted dry ingredients and vanilla. Bake in moderate oven for 20 minutes. Serve with whipped cream or boiled custard.

Mrs. Frank Mathews

Stuffed Angel-food Cake

¼ cup crystalized cherries
1 cup nuts
¼ cup crystalized pineapple
8 marshmallows
1 pt. cream - whipped

Cut fruit in small pieces and let stand over night in Whiskey or La Rosa Sherry Wine. Slice ½" layer off top of cake and scoop out cake leaving a shell. Add nuts marshmallows and bits of cake to fruit mixture. Moisten with half of whipped cream and fill cake. Replace top layer and ice entire cake with remaining sweetened whipped cream. Decorate with crystalized fruit in flower pattern.

Mrs Arthur Mead

Summer Fruit Dessert

3 Cantaloupes — 1 Honey Dew Melon
2 fresh Pineapples — 2 doz. Peaches
1 lb. white seedless grapes (or 2 cans white cherries — remove seeds from these.)

Scoop out cantaloupe and honey dew in round balls. Cut up peaches and pull pineapple off stalk with silver fork (kitchen fork changes color of pineapple.) Wash and add seedless grapes. Add sugar to taste, about 1 cup. After sugar is well mixed with fruit, add several tablespoons of La Rosa Sherry wine and place in ice box to chill. Garnish with fresh red cherries.

Mrs. Walker Smith

Angel Breath

whites of 6 eggs -   ½ tsp. vanilla
1½ cups sugar.   1 tsp. vinegar

Beat whites until stiff. Add sugar gradually - then vanilla, and vinegar. Place in pie pan or muffin tins and bake in a very slow oven 1 hr. Serve with ice cream, fruit, or sauce.

Miss Leila Dowe -

- Apple Float -

1 doz. green (acid) apples - 1 cup sugar
Whites of 4 eggs -   1 tbsp. vanilla

Peel apples, and cook until tender using as little water as possible for apples should be fairly dry. Beat egg whites stiff. Add ½ cup sugar & beat until like meringue. Mix apples, beaten egg whites and rest of sugar. Beat until mixture has more than doubled its quantity. Add vanilla last.

Mrs. Mortimer Tuttle

205.

Queen of Trifles

Make a 3 egg custard in double boiler (using 3 eggs, 1 qt. milk, ½ cup sugar, thickening & vanilla — make quite thick).
Blanch 1 lb. almonds & put through food chopper. Mix with custard & set in refrigerator till next day
1 qt. whipping cream - beaten stiff
1 doz. macaroons - soaked in La Rosa sherry
1 doz. lady fingers - separated
Line bowl with lady fingers layer of custard, layer of macaroons, layer of whipped cream etc... until finished with cream on top. Garnish top with cherries. Serves 10.

Mrs. Frank Zenville Sr.

Chess Cake Pie

8 egg yolks -
2 cups sugar
1 cup melted butter
1 tsp. vinegar
nutmeg
Pinch of salt
Crystallized fruit or citron for garnish

Beat yolks until creamy, adding sugar gradually. Pour in butter and other ingredients. Put in an uncooked pastry and cook slowly until firm.

Mrs. Frank M. Dixon

Angel Food Pie

4 egg whites - ¼ cup sugar
1 tsp. vanilla.

Beat egg whites until almost stiff. Add vanilla - then sugar gradually, beating until meringue will stand in peaks. Pour in a baked pie crust, making center lower. Bake in a 300° oven for 30 minutes until slightly browned.

Use any crushed fruit or berries as filling, topped with 1 cup whipped cream sweetened with ¼ cup sugar.

Mrs. Frank Tripp

Lemon Custard - Banana Pie   207.

3/4 cups sugar
2 Tbsps. corn starch
2 Tbsps. White Lily flour
1/4 tsp. salt

2 egg yolks - beaten lightly
2 cups scalded milk
rind of 1/2 lemon - grated
2 bananas - sliced lengthwise

Mix sugar, corn starch, flour and salt thoroughly. Add egg yolks and milk. Cook in double boiler until thick and smooth. Remove from heat and chill. Place bananas in pie crust. Pour cream filling over bananas and cover top with following meringue: Beat 2 egg whites stiffly, add 4 Tbsps. sugar and 1/2 tsp. lemon juice. Bake golden brown. Serve when cold.

Mrs. Nina Stone

Lemon Chiffon Pie

Beat 4 egg yolks - pinch salt.
½ c hot water - ½ c sugar and cook until thick. Add package Knox gelatine softened in ¼ c cold water.

Beat 4 egg whites stiff. Add ½ c sugar. To custard add juice 2 lemons (grated rind of one) Fold in egg whites and pour in Graham cracker pie crust.

   Mrs. Evelyn Taber

Lemon Custard

1 c sugar   Pinch salt
1 c sweet milk   1 tbsp. White Lily flour
3 eggs   Juice and rind 1 lemon

Beat yolks and sugar together. Add lemon. Put White Lily flour into cup, add milk very slowly dissolving flour. Pour into mixture. Bake in rich, single piecrust using whites with 6 tbsp. sugar for meringe. Place on top of baked pie and brown.

   Mrs. Chas. Gayle Brown

Lemon Pie

1 c water 1 lemon
1 c sugar (take out 2 tbsp. for meringue)
2 eggs 1 tbsp. butter
1 heaping tbsp White Lily Flour

Put sugar and water in saucepan and boil. Add to the well beaten yolks, grated lemon rind, melted butter and flour. Pour on this the boiling mixture — cook until thickens like custard, add lemon juice, let cool. Put into a baked crust, cover with the meringue made of the stiffly beaten whites and 2 tbsp. sugar.

Mrs. John E. Bartlett, Sr.

Butterscotch-chiffon Pie

1 envelope plain gelatine 1 c scalded milk
1/4 c cold water
3 eggs separated 2 tbsp. butter
1 c brown sugar 1/2 tsp. vanilla
  1/4 c granulated sugar
1/4 tsp. salt

Soak gelatine in cold water 5 minutes. Beat yolks and slowly heat in milk. Add butter and salt; cook in double boiler, stirring until custardlike. Stir in gelatine. Cool and add vanilla. Fold in stiffly beaten whites (in which sugar has been beaten). Pour into 9 inch baked pie shell; chill.

Mrs. T. B. Scott

Bread Pudding

2 cups stale bread without crust
1 qt. scalded milk — ½ cup sugar.
3 tbsp. butter — 3 egg yolks —
½ tsp. salt — 1 tsp. vanilla — or
¼ tsp. nutmeg — ½ cup seeded and
shredded raisins.

Soak crumbs in milk; cool slightly; add sugar, butter, and egg yolks, slightly beaten, salt, flavoring, and fruit. Turn mixture into a buttered baking dish and bake one hour in a slow oven. Cover the first 30 minutes of cooking. Cover with meringue made from 3 beaten egg whites and 3 tbsp. granulated sugar. Bake slowly until light brown.

    Mrs. N. J. Bell —

Meringue Pie

Beat stiff whites of 3 eggs and 1 pinch salt. Add 6 tbsp. of sugar. Then beat until sugar is dissolved. Add 1 tbsp. tarragon vinegar.

Butter a nine inch pie pan. Pour in meringue & bake at 270° between 30 or 40 minutes. Turn out on a platter. When cool — crush in top, and pour in crushed strawberries or fresh peaches. Ice with whipped cream & decorate with fruit. Slice like pie.

    Mrs. Fred Caldwell
    Louisville, Ky.

Angel Pie

1 c brown sugar
1 c milk
2 tbsp. butter
1 tsp. vanilla
2 tbsp. White Lily flour
Pie crust

2 eggs
½ tsp. salt
1 tsp. cornstarch
Whipped Cream

Cream sugar and add milk — beat up well together and put in double boiler. Beat eggs separately. To yolks, add White Lily flour, salt and cornstarch. Add this to mixture in boiler and cook until it thickens, stirring all the while.

Cool and fold in the well beaten whites and add vanilla. Put this into the pie crust and top with whipped cream.

Mrs. Walton Hill

212.

Pecan Pie

3 eggs
1 cup brown sugar
1 cup Karo syrup
1 tbsp. butter
1 cup pecans
1 tsp. vanilla

Cream sugar and butter and add syrup, well beaten eggs, pinch of salt and vanilla. When well mixed, add halved pecans and put in pie plate lined with pastry. Bake in moderate oven until firm.

Mrs. Maude McLendon

Amber Pie

1 cup sugar
1 tbsp. White Lily flour
4 eggs
1 tbsp. butter

Cream above ingredients thoroughly and add 1 tsp. cinnamon, ¼ tsp. cloves, nutmeg to flavor, 1 tbsp. vinegar, 1 cup buttermilk, 1 cup seedless raisins. Cook slowly until thick. Pour mixture into a baked pie crust. Cover with meringue and brown delicately.

Mrs. Y. H. Moore

Tyler Pudding Pie
(2 pies)

1 ½ cups white sugar
1 ½ cups brown sugar
1 cup cream   1 cup butter
5 eggs   Vanilla and nutmeg

Melt butter, then put cream and butter in a double boiler. Beat eggs until very light, add them to the cream and butter. Then flavor mixture with vanilla. Pour into uncooked pie crust and sprinkle with nutmeg. Bake in a slow oven until very brown.

— Mrs. W. A. Gunter —

This recipe was used in the White House during the administration of President Tyler, the tenth president of the United States.

Apple Crisp

4 or 5 sour apples
½ cup butter
1 cup brown sugar
1 cup White Lily flour

Fill a buttered glass pie plate with peeled, sliced apples. Cream together butter, sugar and flour. Spread this mixture over apples. Sprinkle top with nutmeg or cinnamon. Cook in hot oven for first 10 min. Reduce to 350° and cook about 20 min. longer. Serve hot with hard sauce or whipped cream.

Mrs. A. B. Tanner
Birmingham, Ala.

Apple Pie

4 sour apples
⅓ cup sugar
¼ tsp. nutmeg
⅛ tsp. salt
1 tsp. butter
juice 1 lemon

Peel and core apples, cut into eighths. Line pie plates with pastry and fill with apples. Mix sugar, nutmeg, salt, and lemon juice, and sprinkle over apples. Dot with butter; add top crust. Bake 45 min.

Mrs. W. L. Sellers

Chocolate Chiffon Pie

1 – 9" baked pie shell
1 envelope plain gelatine
3/4 c cold water
2 oz. cooking chocolate
4 eggs   1 cup sugar
1/4 tsp. salt   1 tsp. vanilla
1/2 cup heavy cream whipped

Soak gelatine in cold water 5 min. Combine 1/2 c cold water and chocolate and heat until melted. Add gelatine and stir until dissolved. Add to egg yolks, beaten, with 1/2 c sugar, salt and vanilla. Cool. When mixture begins to thicken, fold in the egg whites, stiffly beaten with 1/2 c sugar.

Turn into baked pie shell and chill. Spread with whipped cream and serve.

—Mrs. John W. Persons

Pastry – never fails –

2 cups White Lily flour – sifted
1/3 cup Wesson Oil   1/2 Tsp. Salt
1/4 cup water

Sift flour, then measure. Mix oil and water in a cup and stir hard with a fork. Add quickly to the flour and salt. Knead lightly. Divide and roll on a floured board. Bake at 500° for 8 to 12 minutes. This amount makes 2 pie crusts.

Mrs. Roy Nolen

Hot Water Pie Crust

1/2 cup boiling water   1 cup Shortening
3 cups White Lily flour   1 Tsp. Salt

Pour boiling water over fat and salt. Stir until creamy. Add flour, sifted before measuring. Mix thoroughly and chill.

Mrs. P. Warren Tyson

Fruit Sherbet

Dissolve over stove, 3 cups sugar, and 3 cups water. When cool, add 3 bananas, 3 oranges, and 1 pineapple (canned will do). Also the juice of 3 lemons. When the mixture begins to freeze, add the whites of 2 eggs - well beaten. Put the bananas through a colander and chop other fruits fine.

Mrs. M. W. Stuart Sr.

Apricot Sherbet

1 large can apricots - 1 qt. water
juice of 4 lemons - 1½ cups sugar
1 tbsp. Knox gelatine

Boil water with sugar 10 minutes. When slightly cool, add gelatine previously soaked in ½ cup cold water. Mash apricots through colander; add lemon juice and the sugar syrup. Freeze.

Mrs. S. M. Bashinsky
Troy, Alabama

Peppermint Mousse

½ cup creamed Peppermints - crushed.
1 Tsp. gelatin, dissolved in 2 Tbsp. water
1 cup milk
½ Tsp. vanilla
1 cup cream
Salt

Heat milk and add gelatin, then add crushed peppermint and salt. Cool and add flavoring. Turn into open freezing tray. When mixture begins to thicken, turn into bowl and beat until frothy. Beat cream until stiff, fold into above mixture and freeze. Kitty S. Joseph

Frozen Delight Mousse

3 eggs - 2 tbsp. chopped pecans
½ cup sugar - 2 Tbsp. candied cherries
2 tbsp. La Rosa Sherry
1 pt. cream - 1 doz. Lady fingers

Beat yolks of eggs and add sugar until very light. Add sherry; then add the well-beaten egg whites. Add cream, whipped. Line a mold with halves of lady fingers - then pour in the cream mixture, adding pecans and cherries just before putting in mold. Cover mold and pack tightly in ice and salt for 3 or 4 hours.

Mrs. L. L. Hill

Strawberry Sherbet

2 qts. berries - 4 c. water
2 c. sugar - ½ c. lemon juice

Boil sugar and water together 10 min. When cool, add berries that have been put through a sieve. Freeze.

Mrs. J. M. Hobbie -

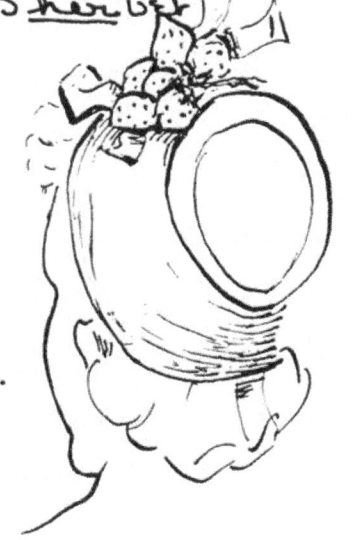

Maple Mousse

Beat 6 egg yolks adding 2 c syrup. Thicken in double boiler. Cool and add 1 qt cream whipped, 6 egg whites stiffly beaten. Pack in ice and salt for 4 hours.

  Mrs. Charles Thigpen Sr.

Coffee Ice Cream

2/3 c Borden's Eagle Brand Sweetened Condensed Milk
1/2 c strong black coffee
1/2 tsp. vanilla
1 c whipping cream

Mix milk, coffee and vanilla. Chill. Whip cream to custard like consistency. Fold into chilled mixture. Freeze in freezing unit of refrigerator until half frozen. Scrape from freezing tray and beat until smooth but not melted. Replace in freezing unit until frozen. Serves 6.

  Mrs. Harris Dawson Sr.

Frozen Grape Juice

1 pt. Welch's grape juice   1 pt. water
1 c sugar   juice of 3 lemons

Bring water and sugar to a boil. Cool. Mix and freeze.

  Mrs. W. A. Bellingrath

Raspberry Sherbet Mold
with Whipped Cream —

1 can red raspberries
Juice of 6 lemons —
1 pt. cream — whipped
1½ cans water
2 cups sugar —

Press raspberries — add lemon juice, water, and sugar and put into a freezing tray until sherbet is frozen hard about ½ inch thick all around the sides. Then hollow out the central portion, replacing it with whipped cream. Put the sherbet that has been scooped out on top of the whipped cream.

Mrs. W. M. Marks Sr.

RASPBERRY SHERBET

Lemon Milk Sherbet

1 pint milk — 1 cup sugar
½ pint whipping cream
Juice of 2 lemons — Rind of 1 lemon (grated)

Stir sugar in lemon juice, then add milk and cream (whipped) and stir well. Set in refrigerator tray to freeze, stirring often.

— Mrs. W. C. Bowman —

Chocolate Ice Cream

16 marshmallows — 3 tbsp. sugar
1 square bitter Chocolate — 1 cup milk
½ pint whipping cream — 1 tsp. vanilla

Steam marshmallows, chocolate and milk in top of double boiler until melted. Add sugar and vanilla. Cool and when cold, fold in stiffly beaten whipped cream. Pour into tray and freeze without stirring.

— Mrs. Wiley Hill, Jr. —

Pineapple-Lime Sherbert

1 package Lemon-Lime Kool-Aid
4 c. sugar   3 c. sweet milk
1 small can crushed pineapple

Mix ingredients and freeze in "hand-turned" freezer. If wish to make in electric refrigerator add 1 c. milk instead of 3 c. milk and freeze to a mush; then add 1 pt. whipping cream and freeze hard.

          Mrs. T. B. Hill Jr.

Ice Cream

1 c. milk   1 c. whipped cream
16 marshmallows

Place milk over hot water and dissolve marshmallows, cool, put in refrigerator and let partially freeze and add whipped cream.

          Mrs. Robert Pinkston

Chocolate Ice Box Pudding

2 cakes German sweet chocolate, melt in double boiler with 5 tsp. water
2 egg yolks
5 tbsp. confectioners sugar
Fold in 2 egg whites stiffly beaten
Add to this 1 c. cream (whipped). Line mold with lady fingers. Pour in chocolate mixture; cover with lady fingers. Chill in refrigerator for 12 hours. Serve with whipped cream. Serves 5 to 6 people.

          Mrs. S. F. Stakely

Macaroon Ice Cream

1 qt. cream whipped stiff.
1 ½ doz. macaroons rolled fine.
1 doz. marshmallows cut up and dissolved in 1 cup milk.
2 tsps. vanilla and 1 cup La Rosa Sherry wine. Sweeten to taste. Mix and put in freezer.

Mrs. W. St. John Mafred

Pineapple Sherbet

1 pint water   Juice of 4 lemons
1 ½ cups sugar   Whites of 2 eggs
1 tsp. gelatin
1 quart unsweetened pineapple juice

Boil water and sugar for a few minutes. Add gelatin soaked in ¼ cup cold water. When mixture cools, add juice and freeze. When half frozen, add whites of 2 eggs beaten stiff.

Mrs. George A. Robbins

Ring Mold for Ice Cream

26 marshmallows melted in double boiler with 1 stick of butter. Mix with 1 box of Rice Crispies and put in buttered ring mold. If the weather is damp, put in refrigerator. Let stand several hours. When ready to use, turn out and serve ice cream in the center.

                Mrs. R. S. Toldthwaite
                Mobile, Ala.

Gingerbread or Plum Pudding Sauce

2 egg yolks ⎤ cream together
1 cup sugar ⎦

2 tbsp. whiskey or rum
1 tsp. vanilla

Whip ½ pt. cream and add to above mixture. Serves 5

                Mrs. Hilton Rice

226.

Sauce for Vanilla Ice Cream

¼ lb. crystallized cherries   1 can Kadota Figs
⅛ lb. crystallized ginger   1 bottle Marrons
2 rings crystallized pineapple ¼ lb. citron

Drain & chop figs - cut cherries in half - cut up ginger & pineapple. Shave citron & quarter Marrons. & jar, then pour either brandy or whiskey (Rye or Bourbon) over to taste and to make it the consistency of a sauce. Serve over vanilla ice cream

        Mrs. Temple Seibels

Egg Nog Sauce for Ice Cream

2 eggs   2 tbsp. sugar
¼ cup whiskey   ½ pint cream
1 tsp. Jamaica Rum   1 tsp. La Rosa sherry

Beat egg yolks 10 mins. Add sugar slowly. Pour whiskey into mixture; beat 5 mins. more. Add rum and sherry wine. Fold in stiffly beaten egg whites & whipped cream. Keep on ice till ready to serve.

    Mrs. John Martin

Orange Sauce

4 egg yolks   1 tbsp. lemon juice
1 cup sugar   grated rind of 1½ oranges
juice of 2 oranges   2 cups thick cream

Beat yolks light; add sugar gradually, beat till light & foamy; add juices & rind. Cook in double boiler, stirring constantly until quite thick. Set aside to cool. Whip cream till frothy but not dry, and add cooled mixture gradually. This will keep for several days. Extra good on gingerbread or chocolate pudding.

    Mrs. Geo. Cleaderick
    Quartermaster Corps., U.S.A.

Cakes · Cookies and Icings

Grandma's Pound Cake –

6 eggs –   1 ¾ cups sugar –
1 cup butter –   ½ tsp. nutmeg (more
                          if desired)
2½ cups White Lily flour –

     Cream butter and sugar.
Beat in one egg at a time until
all six are used – alternating
with flour. Pour in a
greased stem loaf pan.
"Elbow grease" is what makes
this cake good.

         Mrs. Frank M. Dixon –

Date Cake

6 packages dates
1/4 lb. candied cherries
3 cups White Lily flour
1 scant cup butter
1 Tsp. vanilla
1 lb. pecans
1/2 lb. citron
6 eggs
2 cups sugar
1/2 cup whiskey

2 rounding Tsps. baking powder

Chop nuts and fruit and mix with other ingredients. Pack in large cake pan and bake 3 to 4 hours.

— Mrs. Winfrey Oliver —

Almond Cake

1 lb. almonds
1 doz. eggs
1 lb. sugar

Put unskinned almonds through fine chopper. Beat eggs separately, add sugar to yolks, add almonds and last the well-beaten whites. Bake in moderate oven (350°) for 1 hour and 10 minutes.

— Mrs. E. H. Pritchett —
Tuscaloosa, Alabama

Chop Suey Cake

½ cup. Crisco — 1 tsp. cinnamon.
1½ cups sugar — ½ tsp. nutmeg.
2 cups sour milk — 1 pinch salt.
2 heaping tbsp. cocoa — 1 cup raisins
1 tsp. ginger — 1 cup nut meats
1 tsp. cloves — 2 cups White Lily
2 tsp. soda   flour

Mix Crisco and sugar. Add spices and cocoa — then sour milk, soda, flour, raisins, and nuts. Bake in a medium oven using a square pan. Caramel or coffee icing may be used.

Aileen M. Sorensen.
Maxwell Field —

Sponge Cake

6 egg whites — 6 egg yolks.
1¼ cups White Lily Flour —
2 tsp. orange flavor
⅓ cup water
1¼ cups sugar
1 tsp. cream tartar
¼ tsp. salt.

Cook sugar and water until it forms a soft ball. Pour over beaten whites like an icing. Beat until cold, and pour over it the well-beaten yolks. Then fold in the flour, into which the salt and cream of tartar have been sifted. Flour the pan and cook 1 hour. Use Angel food pan. Ice with orange icing.

    Mrs. F. P. Pointer

— "Land of the Sky" Cake —

Cream until light 2 cups sugar and 1 cup of butter. Add: 5 eggs beaten together — ½ cup. molasses 1 cup sour milk — ¼ cup melted chocolate 1 tsp soda (dissolved in sour milk) 3 cups sifted White Lily flour 2 tsp. vanilla — 1 cup pecans 1 cup chopped raisins.

 Bake in layer cake pans and put together with boiled frosting. Between layers — after icing — sprinkle shredded pineapple which has been thoroughly drained.

    Mrs. C. G. Hume —

Raisin Cake

1 package seeded raisins
2 cups brown sugar
½ cup butter
2 whole eggs
4 cups white Lily flour
1 tsp. vanilla
1 tsp. soda
1 tsp. baking powder
Spices if desired – but not necessary.

Cover raisins with water and boil until 1 cup of liquid remains – about 20 minutes. Cool and strain off liquid. Cream butter and sugar. Add beaten eggs and beat well. Add raisins. Add soda to raisin water, holding over bowl as it will run over. Stir in flour to which baking powder has been added and add vanilla. Pour into well greased pan and bake about 1 hour in a moderate oven.

The addition of nut meats and crystalized fruits makes a very delicious fruit cake. Can also be served with a wine sauce for an unusual dessert.

Mrs. Owen Brown

Cruellers

6 eggs -
2 scant cups sugar
¾ cup butter

Beat eggs separately. To sugar, add butter creamed, add yolks, and then beaten whites. Add enough White Lily Flour to make a stiff dough - or the cruellers will not fry well. Fry in deep fat hot enough to brown the dough but not to burn it. Drain on paper. Sprinkle with powdered sugar.

Mrs. W. A. Bellingrath.

For Special Recipes

For Special Recipes

Lemon and Pineapple Cake

8 egg whites   2 cups sugar
1 cup sweet milk   1/2 lb. butter
1 heaping tsp. baking powder
3 cups White Lily Flour
1 tsp. vanilla

Cream butter and sugar, add sweet milk, then flour, and baking powder sifted 3 times. Fold in egg whites and put in 3 well greased cake pans with paper in pans.

Filling

Small can pineapple (crushed)
1 cup sugar
8 egg yolks
juice of 2 lemons and rind
2 tbsp. butter

Beat egg yolks, add cup sugar and can of pineapple, also juice of 2 lemons and a little grated rind. Cook until thick in double boiler. Spread between layers and on top of cake.

         Mrs. Robert Anderson

Graham Cracker Cake

1 medium sized box Graham Crackers
1 cup sugar
1/2 cup butter
3/4 cup milk
1 cup pecans
1 tsp. baking powder
2 eggs

Cream butter, sugar and add egg yolks. Roll and sift crackers, add baking powder alternately with milk, then tsp. vanilla. Bake in slow oven in layer pans.

Icing

3 tbsp. cocoa
3 tbsp. strong coffee
2 tbsp. butter
1 box XXXX sugar
Enough cream to spread easily.

Mrs. Curtis Nordan

Pineapple Upside Down Cake

½ cup butter   1 cup brown sugar
1 medium size can pineapple
Melt butter in large baking pan & sprinkle sugar evenly over this. Arrange slices of pineapple on the sugar & cover with following cake mixture:

3 eggs   1 cup White Lily flour
1 cup sugar   1 tsp. baking powder
5 tbsp pineapple juice   pinch of salt

Beat egg yolks & then cream with sugar. Add pineapple juice. Sift in flour in which has been mixed baking powder & salt. Fold in stiffly beaten egg whites & pour over the pineapple. Bake in a moderate (375°) oven about 30 mins.

  Mrs. G. B. Cleveland

Yellow Cake

Yolk 14 eggs
1/2 lb. butter
2 cups sugar
3 1/2 cups White Lily flour
3 teaspoons baking powder
1 1/4 cups milk
1 teaspoon vanilla

Cream butter and sugar. Sift flour before measuring, then add baking powder and mix with butter and sugar, alternately with milk. Add yolks of eggs that have been beaten until they are thick and lemon colored. Add vanilla. Put in greased and floured angel food pan and cook in 325° oven for about 1 hr.

Mrs. W. H. Hackney

Blackberry Jam Cake

2 cups sugar
6 eggs
1 full Tsp. soda
2 Tsps. allspice
2 Tsps. Cinnamon

1 1/3 cups butter
6 Tbsps. buttermilk
2 Tsps. cloves
2 Tsps. nutmeg
2 cups jam, added last.

4 cups White Lily flour, measured before sifting.

Cream butter and sugar until light. Add whole eggs, one at a time, buttermilk in which soda has been dissolved. Sift flour with spices and add slowly to first mixture. Add jam last. Bake in layer cake pans and ice with boiled frosting.

Mrs. C. S. Hume

Grooms Cake

12 eggs - separated and beaten -
½ cup toasted, sifted bread crumbs -
1 tsp. salt - 2 tsp. vanilla - 1 cup nuts
Grated rind of 1 orange
Grated rind of 1 lemon
Juice of ½ orange - juice of 1 lemon
10 tbsp. whiskey or brandy

    Mix pecans - rinds of orange and lemon and bread crumbs. Mix orange juice, lemon juice, vanilla, and whiskey. Add dry ingredients to egg yolks; then add liquids. Add salt to beaten whites, and add slowly to egg yolk batter. Pour into greased Spring Cake form. Set oven at 275°, 10 minutes before putting in cake. After cake has cooked 15 minutes set oven at 300° - then 350°. Bake about one hour.

- Icing for Grooms Cake -

1 cup cream - 1 tbsp. butter
1 tsp. vanilla - 1 cup white sugar
2 cups dark brown sugar

    Cook until syrup will form

a soft ball in cold water. Beat and pour over cake before it begins to set. Decorate with halves of pecans - crystalized cherries, and pineapple. Serves 20 to 24 slices.

   Mrs. Sidney G. Weil

- Angel Food Cake -

Add a pinch of salt to eight egg whites and beat until frothy. Add one teaspoon of cream of tartar, and beat until stiff but not dry. Fold in 1 cup of sugar which has been sifted. Sift 3/4 cup of White Lily Flour 5 times. Fold in batter - but do not beat. Flavor with one teaspoon of vanilla. Bake in an oven of 275 or 300 degrees about one hour. Invert, and when cold, serve either with icing or not as preferred.

   Mrs. Frank McPherson -

244 – Chocolate Angel Food Cake

1 1/4 cups egg whites   1/4 tsp. salt
1 tsp. cream of tartar
1 1/2 cups fine sifted sugar
3/4 cup cake flour sifted before
                        measuring
1/4 cup cocoa   1/4 tsp. vanilla
      1/2 tsp. lemon extract

Beat egg whites with salt until frothy. Add cream of tartar and beat stiff, but not dry. Fold in sugar 1 tbsp. at a time, using circular motion. Gradually fold in flour and color, sifted to-245 gether 5 times. Fold in flavoring. Do not beat. Bake in angel cake pan, starting in cold oven and letting the thermometer go to 275-300°. Bake about 1 or 1 1/4 hours. When firm to touch, invert in pan and let cake hang until cool.

~ Icing ~

2 egg whites   1 1/2 cups sugar
1 1/2 Tsps. Karo syrup   5 Tbsps. water
1 kitchen spoon Hyprolite   pinch salt
         vanilla and lemon juice

Put in double boiler and beat with rotary beater for 7 minutes. If icing is soft, continue beating after it is removed from heat until right consistency is reached.

Mrs. Frank McPherson

246 -
Yellow Angel Food Cake

12 egg yolks
¼ teaspoon salt
½ cup cold water
1 cup sugar
1½ cup White Lily flour
1 teaspoon extract
2 teaspoons baking powder

    Place egg yolks, salt, and water in bowl and beat until they hold up well. Then beat in sugar. Fold in flour, add extract and bake like white angel food cake.

          Mrs. S. D. Sawyer

Velvet Sponge Cake

6 eggs
3 cups sifted White Lily flour
1 cup boiling water
2 cups sugar
½ teaspoon salt

    Beat yolks a little, then add sugar and boiling water, beat until stiff and lemon colored. Add 3 level teaspoons baking powder to flour and sift again. Add yolk mixture and stir. Fold in stiffly beaten whites last.

          Mrs. W. B. Nelson

English Ginger Cake

2 cups White Lily Flour –
1 tsp. soda – 2 tbsp. syrup –
1 tsp. cinnamon – 1 stick butter
1 cup brown sugar – 2 eggs –
¼ tsp. cloves – 1 package of raisins
slightly cut up.
Mix and bake as you would any
other cake. Will keep in ice box
indefinitely – and the older it
gets, the better it tastes.

Mrs. Michael Cody –

– Hazelnut Cake –

2 lbs. nuts – 9 tbsp. sugar
9 eggs – 1 Tsp. vanilla
1 tsp. baking powder –

Beat yolks and add sugar.
Beat whites stiff. Add nuts
and whites of eggs and sugar.
Add 1 tbsp. cinnamon. Work
well together. Let stand ½
hr. to rise. Then bake.

Miss Lula Wyman –

White Fruit Cake

1 lb. white raisins — ½ lb. citron
1 lb. candied pineapple — 1 lb. candied cherries
¼ lb. mixed orange and lemon peel
1 lb. nut meats — 1 cup shortening
3 cups White Lily flour, sifted
1 cup granulated sugar — 5 eggs —
¼ tsp. salt — 2 tsp. baking powder
⅓ cup fruit juice — 1½ tbsp. vanilla

Cut up fruits and nuts coarsely and mix thoroughly with 1 cup flour. Cream shortening — gradually add sugar and cream well. Add eggs — one at a time — beating vigorously after each addition. Sift remaining 2 cups of flour with salt and baking powder and add to mixture alternately with the fruit juice and vanilla extract. Fold in the floured fruits and nut meats.

Mrs. Carl Cooper

Glorified Fudge Cake

2 squares Baker's Chocolate
3 eggs   1/8 tsp. soda
1/2 stick butter   1/8 tsp. baking powder
1 cup sugar   1 cup nuts
2/3 cups White Lily flour   1 tsp. vanilla

Melt butter & chocolate together in double boiler. Remove from heat, add sugar & eggs, & beat well. Into this sift flour, baking powder & soda. Pour into shallow pan & bake in a slow oven. When done & while still hot, cover with marshmallows. Turn off heat & leave cake in oven till marshmallows have become very soft. When cool & while still in the pan, cover cake with any good chocolate icing. Cut into squares.

       Mrs. Thos. H. Edwards

Pound Cake

2 cups butter — 2 cups sugar
4 cups White Lily flour
2 tsp. baking powder — 10 eggs
4 tbsp. water — vanilla extract

Cream butter and sugar together well; mix in water. Beat eggs together and add half at a time. Add flour in the same manner.

Mrs. C. L. Marks —

— White Cake —

2/3 cup Snowdrift — 2 cups sugar
1 cup lukewarm water — 8 egg whites
3½ cups White Lily flour —
4 tsp. baking powder — 1 tsp. vanilla
1 tsp. almond flavoring — ¼ tsp. salt.

Cream Snowdrift and sugar. Add flour sifted with baking powder, alternating with water. Last — fold in eggs which have been beaten with salt until stiff but not dry. Bake in a moderate oven.

Mrs. Robert Teague Sr.

Honey Cakes

4 eggs
2 cups brown sugar
2 cups White Lily flour
2 cups coarsely chopped pecans
2 tsp. baking powder
1 pkg. pitted chopped dates
1 tsp. powdered cloves
1 tsp. cinnamon
1 tsp. allspice

Beat eggs till light, add brown sugar, beat till smooth. Add spices, flour, baking powder, nuts, dates & spread in greased biscuit tin to ½ in. thickness. Bake in moderate oven, 350°, till brown. Take out and spread with Bakers* icing while hot & cut in 1½ in. squares when cool. Cakes are better after being kept in a tin box 2 days.

*Bakers icing: Add 3 Tbsp. cream & ½ tsp. vanilla to 1 cup powdered sugar. Beat till well blended.

Mrs. Frank Harvey Miller

Pecan Cake

1 lb. white sugar - 1 cup brown sugar
1 lb. White Lily Flour - ¾ lb. butter
6 eggs beaten whole - 1½ lbs. pecans -
1½ lbs. raisins - ½ pt. whiskey -
1½ grated nutmegs - 2 tsp. baking powder

Cream butter and sugar. Add eggs. Dredge nuts and raisins in flour and add. Sift baking powder & flour. Grate nutmeg into whiskey. Mix all and bake 3 hours or a little longer. Keep in pan until cold. Then pour a little whiskey over the cake.

Mrs. R. R. Russell.

Lemon Cheese Filling

1½ lemons - juice & rind
½ stick butter
1½ cups sugar (sift before measuring)
yolks of 9 eggs (drop in a little water)

Cream lemon juice, rind, sugar, and butter. Add yolks. Continue beating. Cook in a double boiler until very thick. Be sure to continue beating to prevent ingredients from separating.

Mrs. Frank Charlt
Mr. Meigs - Ala.

Cocoanut Icing

2 cups sugar
½ cup water
Whites of 4 eggs
½ cup sugar
1 tsp vanilla
juice of 1 lemon.

Cook sugar and water until it spins a thread. Beat whites stiff, add ½ cup sugar slowly. Add syrup and vanilla. When it stands firm, add lemon juice. Spread on layer of cake and sprinkle thick with grated fresh cocoanut. Then next thing. Place second layer on top and do likewise.
      Mrs. E. C. Dickson.

Chocolate Icing

Thin 1 package cream cheese with 3 tbsp heavy cream. Add pinch of salt and vanilla flavoring to taste. Work in 1 box Confectioners sugar. Melt 3 squares of bitter chocolate and add to mixture.
      Mrs. Ed. Fowler.

Lane Cake Filling

Beat well together yolks of 8 eggs, 1 heaping cup sugar - and ½ cup butter. Cook over hot water until thick, stirring constantly. When done, and while still hot, pour in 1 cup chopped raisins 1 cup coconut, 1 pound English walnuts, 1 wine glass La Rosa wine or brandy, and 1 teaspoon vanilla. Use filling between layers, and seven minute icing on top and sides of the cake.

Mrs. M. H. Pearson -

Devils Food Cake Icing

½ cup. butter
1 package powdered sugar.
1 egg yolk -
4 tbsp. cocoa
5 tbsp. warm coffee.

Mix all ingredients in the order given.

Mrs. F. H. Marshall -

~ Caramel Filling ~

3 cups sugar   1 cup milk
1 cup butter   3 Tbsp. white lily flour

Cook sugar, flour and butter until it begins to brown. Add milk and cook until very thick. Take from stove and beat until cool, then spread on cake.

~ Mrs. A. Hornsby ~
Ain Coys ~

~ Orange Icing ~

1 1/2 lbs. xxxx sugar   2 egg yolks
Juice and rind of 1 or 2 oranges, cooked at least 20 minutes and then strained.
1/2 stick soft butter ~

Beat eggs well, add to juice, then sugar and butter. Few grains of salt and a little lemon juice. Make soft enough to spread.

~ Mrs. H. B. Bowers ~
New Orleans ~

Chocolate Cream Roll

6 eggs
½ cup cocoa
½ cup granulated sugar
1 tsp. vanilla
¼ cup confectioners sugar
½ tsp. baking powder
½ cup sifted White Lily flour
pinch of salt

Beat egg yolks very light. Add salt to egg whites, beat stiff & dry. Then fold in confectioners sugar. Mix well, fold in sifted sugar & cocoa. Fold cocoa mixture lightly into well beaten egg yolks. Add vanilla. Sift in flour & baking powder together, & fold in lightly. Turn mixture into well greased biscuit pan lined with heavy waxed paper. Bake in moderate oven, 350°, about 25 mins. — Turn cake out on damp cloth or one that has been rubbed with flour. Peel off waxed paper quickly & roll up cake like jelly roll in cloth or towel. Let cool then open and spread quickly with sweetened whipped cream. Roll up cake again

and let it stand 1 hr. before serving.
Roll may be covered with chocolate
icing if desired.
    Mrs. Charles F. Moritz

Skillet Cake

½ lb. brown sugar ¼ lb. butter
1 can peaches (or other fruit)
1 cup of nuts (if desired)
Melt brown sugar & butter in iron
skillet, drain fruit of all syrup and
put in skillet. Add nuts.
Make batter of:
2 eggs   ½ cup sweet milk
1 cup sugar   2 cups sifted White Lily flour
½ cup butter   1 tsp. baking powder
Add batter to mixture in skillet.
Put in slow oven to bake nearly 1 hr.
Invert on platter. Serve with whipped
cream, ice cream or syrup of fruit
thickened & sweetened.
    Mrs. Robert Pinkerton

Devil's Food Cake

½ cup cocoa   1 tsp. soda
½ cup hot water   1 pinch salt
1 stick butter   1 cup brown sugar
1 cup white sugar   ½ cup sour milk
1 tsp. baking powder   yellows 3, 4, or 5 eggs
2 cups White Lily flour, sifted

Cream butter and sugar thoroughly. Add egg yolks. Mix baking powder with flour. Add to mixture alternately with milk. Add this mixture to cocoa, soda, water and salt which has been mixed and cooling while mixing batter.

Mrs. J. Hardin
Mr. Graham

Chocolate Cake

2½ cups White Lily flour.
¼ tsp. salt – 1 tsp. soda – 1 cup butter –
2 cups sugar – 5 well beaten eggs –
1 cup nuts – 1 cup buttermilk –
2 tsp. vanilla – 3 squares chocolate
(melted and cooled).

Measure and sift flour with salt and soda. Cream butter and sugar. Add eggs, nuts, melted chocolate, White Lily flour, and milk. Bake in a loaf in oven at 325° for 1 hr.

Mrs. Joe Ledbetter

– Date Loaf –

1 lb. seedless dates – 1 stick butter –
1 cup sugar – 1 cup chopped nuts.
2 cups White Lily flour –
1 tsp. vanilla – 1 tsp. cinnamon –
1 tsp. nutmeg – 3 well beaten eggs

Cream sugar and butter. Add eggs – then White Lily flour, nuts, dates, and vanilla. Bake in a loaf pan 30 minutes in a slow oven.

Mrs. Thomas Martin

Chocolate Cake

1 cup sugar   pinch of salt
⅓ cup butter   scant ½ cup water
1 tsp. cream of tartar   ½ tsp. soda
2 eggs   2 sqr. chocolate
1 heaping cup White Lily flour

Cream butter & sugar. Add cream of tartar, egg yolks, pinch of salt. Put soda in water & add. Then add melted chocolate. Sift in flour. Add last 2 well beaten egg whites. Bake in square flat tins about 25 to 30 minutes.

Icing: 1 cup sweet milk
       1 heaping cup sugar

Boil slowly until it forms a waxy ball in water. Remove from stove, add butter size of walnut & beat a little. When cool, add 2 squares melted chocolate & beat till thick & creamy.

Miss Katherine Baldwin

Little Gold Cakes.

1 cup sugar — 2/3 cup butter
1/2 cup milk   3 tsp. baking powder
1 1/2 cups White Lily flour
8 egg yolks —

Cream butter and sugar well and add 1 tsp. vanilla and 1 tsp. orange juice. Sift baking powder in flour and add milk to butter and sugar. Beat thoroughly and add egg yolks, well-beaten, last. Bake until light brown. Shake powdered sugar over cakes while hot.

Mrs. T. Brannon Hubbard

— Brown Sugar Cup Cakes —

2 eggs —   1 cup brown sugar
1/2 cup White Lily flour — 1/2 tsp. salt
1/2 tsp. baking powder — 1 cup pecans

Beat eggs well. Add sugar, sifted flour and other ingredients. Cook in a muffin pan for ten minutes in a quick oven.

Mrs. H. S. Houghton.

Nestles Chocolate Cookies

2 sticks butter
3/4 cup brown sugar } cream
3/4 cup white sugar
2 eggs

Dissolve 1 tsp. soda in 1 tsp. water. Add 2 1/4 cups White Lily flour, 1 tsp. salt, 1 tsp. vanilla, 1 cup nuts, 2 - 1 oz bars Nestles chocolate broken the size of peas.

Mrs. Don Bryan

Ice Box Cookies

1 cup butter
2 cups brown sugar
2 cups White Lily flour
3 eggs
2 cups chopped nuts
1 tsp. vanilla

Cream butter with sugar and add well beaten eggs. Add sifted flour, nuts and vanilla. Mix well and make into rolls. Wrap in waxed paper and leave in refrigerator over night. Slice and bake in moderate oven.

Mrs. W. W. Bowman

"Brownies"

2 eggs - beaten slightly
1¼ cup brown sugar
1 cup White Lily flour
1 stick butter
½ teasp vanilla
2 squares unsweetened, melted chocolate
½ cup walnuts or pecans chopped.

Mix well and spread evenly in buttered pan - Bake 20 minutes.

   Mrs Keller Humphrey

÷ Date Cookies =

1 well-packed cup brown sugar
¾ cup butter — 1½ cup White Lily flour — 1 cup nuts
2 eggs - 1 package pitted dates

Cream butter and sugar - Add eggs (one at a time) Add chopped nuts and dates. Add flour. Drop on cookie sheet and bake in 350° oven, til brown around edges. Then brown under light.

   Mrs Charles Johnson

Oatmeal Cookies

1 cup sugar
1 cup Crisco   } cream this thoroughly
2 eggs

then add 1 large package dates (first chip dates fine and cover with 1 cup boiling water to which 1 tsp. soda has been added)
1 package seeded raisins — (soak raisins overnight in ha Rosa wine or whiskey)
2 cups sifted White Lily flour
2 cups 3 min. oatmeal
1 tsp. salt
1/3 tsp. each — cloves, cinnamon, allspice
1/2 cup honey   1 1/2 cups pecans
1 slice crystalized pineapple chopped.

Beat all this until well mixed. Better to let stand in ice box until next day before cooking. Cook in moderate oven on a well greased cookie tin —

— Mrs. John Tullis

Sand Tarts

½ lb. butter
5 heaping tbsp. confectioners sugar
1½ cups ground nuts (pecans)
1 tsp. vanilla
2 cups White Lily flour

Mix then mold into little crescents. Put in a greased tin & bake very slowly (250°) about ½ hr. They will not brown, but will be done. When cool, sift powdered sugar on them.

   Mrs. A. J. McLemore

Peanut Butter Cookies

1 stick butter   1 cup peanut butter
2 cups brown sugar   1 tsp. soda
2 eggs   3 cups White Lily flour

Cream butter & sugar. Add eggs & peanut butter. Add soda in last cup of flour. Work into a stiff dough. Pinch off small amounts & roll into marble-size balls. Place on cookie tin. Press balls flat with fork prongs. Cook in moderate oven.

   Mrs. W. W. Brame

266 - ## Bernice's Cookies

2 1/4 cups sugar   3 egg whites
1 tsp. vanilla   1/4 cup water
1 tsp. almond extract
1 1/2 cups chopped pecans
2 cups rolled graham crackers
1/4 tsp. cream of tartar
Small pinch of salt

Cook 2 cups sugar and water into thick syrup. Beat egg whites, salt and cream of tartar stiff. Then beat in 1/4 cup sugar. Add syrup gradually, continuing beating. Fold in vanilla and almond flavoring, graham crackers and nuts. Line pan with oiled paper. Drop mixture from teaspoon and cook in moderate oven about 350° for 40 minutes.

— Mrs. Allen Hopkins —

Toffee Cookies

1 cup shortening - 1 cup brown sugar - 1 egg - 1 tsp. vanilla - 2 cups White Lily Flour - 2 tsp. salt - 2 tsp. cinnamon - ½ cup ground pecans or walnuts.

Cream shortening and brown sugar. Add unbeaten egg yolk and vanilla. Sift flour, salt, and cinnamon - adding a little at a time and blending well. Pat out to ¼ inch thickness on a greased tin. Brush top of mixture with unbeaten egg white and sprinkle with nuts. Bake 30 minutes at 275°. Remove from oven and mark in squares with knife. Remove when cool.

Mrs. Ed. Crosland -

Date Sticks

2 eggs, beaten separately   1 c. pecans
5 level tbs. White Lily Flour   1 c. dates
3/4 c. sugar   1 tsp. vanilla
1 tsp. baking powder

Mix yolks and sugar. Sift flour and baking powder together. Add flour, nuts, and dates to yolks and sugar, a little at a time, then vanilla and beaten egg whites. If mixture is too stiff, add white of another egg. Pour into long or square pan which has been greased and floured. Bake 45 minutes in a slow oven.

        Mrs. Nicholas Pray

Walnut Macaroons

Whites of 6 eggs beaten to a stiff froth, add 1 pound of pulverized sugar and continue to beat for 30 minutes. Stir in 1 pound of black walnuts (cut up very fine). Drop by teaspoonfuls on paper spread on baking pan and bake in a very moderate oven.

        Mrs. Grace Gunter Lane

Frosted Lady Fingers

12 lady fingers - 1/3 cup tart jelly
1 egg white - 1 cup chopped nuts
1 to 2 cups Confectioners sugar

Split lady fingers - spread with jelly - and put halves back together. Add sugar gradually to unbeaten eggs and salt, using enough sugar to make icing of spreading consistency. Add vanilla. Frost lady fingers on all sides. Roll in chopped nuts. Place on waxed paper until dry.

Mrs. John Harris.

Corn Flake Cookies

Whites of 4 eggs - 2/3 cup white sugar
1/3 cup brown sugar - 1 cup pecans
1 ten cent box corn flakes.

Beat egg whites until completely dry. Gradually fold in sugar, Corn Flakes, and nuts. Drop on cookie sheet and bake slowly.

Mrs. Frank Ridolphi

270 -

Almond Strips

Cream 1 stick butter and ¼ lb. powdered sugar. Add 3 whole eggs, one at a time. Then add ½ lb. White Lily Flour. Stir til smooth. Add 1 tsp. vanilla and spread very thinly in pan. Sprinkle top with blanched almonds. Cook in moderate oven 15 min. Cut in strips before cool.

Mrs John P. Kohn

= Chocolate Fudge Cake =

4 eggs 2 cups nuts
1 cup butter 6 tbsp. cocoa
2 cup sugar 1½ cup white Lily Flour

Cream butter and sugar Add whole eggs one at a

time. Sift flour and cocoa and add slowly. Add nuts. Bake in shallow pan in moderate oven. Cut in squares while warm.

Mrs. L. D. Rouse

= Delicious Cookies =

Beat 2 whites of eggs and add 1 cup light brown sugar sifted with 2 rounded tbsp. White Lily Flour. Add 1½ cups chopped pecans or walnuts. Flavor with vanilla. Drop a teaspoon at a time, 1½ in. apart on well greased pan and bake in moderate oven.

Annie Mercer Haynes

Kisses

4 egg whites
1 cup granulated sugar
2 cups nuts
2 tsp. vanilla
pinch salt

Beat egg whites, adding sugar, salt, and vanilla. Beat until the mixture stands alone in peaks, then add nuts and drop spoonsful of this on brown paper and bake slowly.

Mrs. T. B. Hill

Brown Sugar Cookies

½ cup butter
1 cup brown sugar
1 egg
1 cup White Lily flour
1 rounding tsp. baking powder
1 cup nuts
1 tsp. vanilla

Cook butter, sugar, and egg until thick. Let cool and add other ingredients. Drop mixture (about the size of a quarter) onto cookie sheet. Bake in moderate oven.

Drop Cookies

Cream 1/3 cup butter, 2/3 cup brown sugar and 1 egg until fluffy. Sift 1 cup White Lily flour, 1/2 tsp. each of cinnamon, nutmeg and clove, 1/3 tsp. soda and combine with the egg mixture. Add 1/2 cup raisins and 1 cup nuts. Drop by teaspoon on a greased baking sheet and bake in moderate oven 350°.

Mrs. Humphrey Bowling

Nut Squares

1 cup butter   1 cup nuts (broken)
2 cups White Lily flour 1 tsp. ice water
4 tbsps. powdered sugar 1 tbsp. vanilla

Cream sugar and butter and add other ingredients. Work like biscuit dough. Roll out, cut in squares and bake in a quick oven. Roll in powdered sugar.

Mrs. Marion Rushton

Chinese Chews

3/4 cup White Lily Flour - 1/4 tsp. salt.
1 cup sugar - 1 cup chopped pecans -
2 eggs - 1 cup chopped dates

Beat eggs well; then add sugar, flour, and salt - mixing well - then the nuts. Spread on a shallow, greased baking tin. Bake in a moderate oven, and when done, cut in squares.

Mrs. Gordon Meriwether

Chocolate Cookies

1/2 cup butter - 1 cup sugar - 1 egg -
2 squares melted chocolate - 1/3 tsp. salt -
2 cups White Lily Flour - 1 1/2 tsp. Royal Baking Powder - 1 tbsp. cream if needed.

Cream butter and sugar; add eggs, chocolate, and sifted dry ingredients. Roll thin; cut into rounds and bake in a hot oven. Chopped nuts may be added.

Miss Elizabeth McGehee

Chocolate Drops

3/4 cake Dot's chocolate - 1 can Dime Brand condensed milk - 1 can moist coconut - 1 cup chopped nuts. Melt chocolate in double boiler. Add other ingredients. Drop on buttered pan & bake in slow oven 10 to 15 min.

Mrs. Lyle Hinds

Divinity Candy

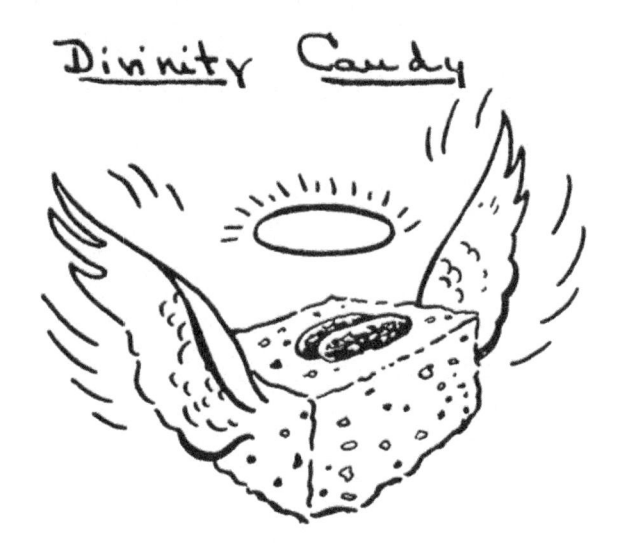

3 cup sugar
½ cup water
1 cup nuts
vanilla

½ cup Karo
2 eggs - whites
pinch salt
cream of tartar

Cook sugar, water and syrup together until it begins to thicken and do not stir.

Have whites beaten stiff and add cream of tartar, pour the syrup slowly, beating all the time, over the beaten whites. Add nuts and tsp. vanilla.

Beat until it begins to thicken and pour out on a buttered dish or marble.

Mrs. Cassie Garrett

Caramel Candy

Caramelize ½ cup white sugar, stirring constantly until it becomes thick syrup. Mix 1½ cups sugar, ½ cup milk, pinch of salt and 1 rounded Tbsp. butter and cook until it boils. Add caramelized sugar, stirring until blended and cook until soft ball stage. Add 1 cup nuts and 1 tsp. vanilla. Beat until creamy.

Mrs. Moss Stuart, Jr.

Pineapple Fudge

1 cup evaporated milk (undiluted)
3 cups sugar
¼ cup pineapple juice
2 Tbsp. butter
2 Tsp. lemon juice

Combine milk, sugar and pineapple juice, cook to soft ball stage, stirring constantly. Add butter and cool in pan without stirring. When cool, add lemon juice and beat until crystallization begins. Pour in buttered pan and cut as desired. For variation ½ cup nuts or crystallized pineapple may be added.

Caramels

3 lbs. sugar
2 lbs. white syrup
1 qt. thin cream
1 qt. whipping cream
1 tbsp. paraffin

Cook sugar, syrup and cream until it forms a soft ball, stirring constantly. Add whipping cream and cook at 246°. Add paraffin and remove from stove. Add 1 tbsp. vanilla, 1 qt. nut meats. Pour into buttered pans 1 inch deep. Let stand over night. Cut in squares and wrap in waxed paper. Makes 8 lbs. candy. Will keep 3 months. — Mrs. John Martin

Buttermilk Candy

2 cups sugar
1 stick butter
1 cup buttermilk
pinch salt
1 tsp. soda
3 tbsp. white Karo syrup
1 cup nuts
1 tbsp. vanilla

Cream sugar and butter, buttermilk, and soda. Add syrup, pinch of salt. Put on fire in large vessel and stir constantly until it forms a soft ball. Add nuts and vanilla. Remove from fire and let cool. Beat well and pour into pan. — Corrie Hill Tankersly

French Candy

1 box Confectioner's sugar
1 tsp. pistachio flavoring
White of 1 egg
Same amount of Cream

Sift sugar. Place white of egg in glass. Add equal amount of cream and a scant ½ tsp. green coloring. Stir well with silver spoon, adding sugar slowly. Keep adding sugar until it becomes a paste thick enough to roll into balls in palm of hand. Roll into pieces about size and shape of pecans and stick whole pecans on each side.

Majorie Allen

Peanut Brittle

3 c. sugar
1 c. white corn syrup
1 lb. raw peanuts (2 c.)
2 tbs. butter

1 c. water
¼ tsp. salt
1 tsp. vanilla
2 tsp. soda

Cook sugar, syrup, water and salt until a firm ball is formed when dropped into water. Now add raw peanuts and cook until brittle when dropped into water. Add butter. Remove from fire and add vanilla and then soda. Stir well and pour into well buttered shallow dish. Begin at once pulling out bits from the sides. Keep pieces as large as possible. Should be very thin and very crisp.

Mrs. W. Boyd McGehee

Chocolate Fudge

Mix 3 cups sugar and 1 scant cup cocoa. Add 3 Tbsps. Karo syrup and 1 cup sweet milk. Add water if too stiff. Boil slowly a drop of the mixture forms a ball when put in water. Turn off gas, add ½ stick butter and 10 marshmallows. Stir until smooth, then beat until ready to pour into buttered pan. When cool, cut in squares.

Mrs. Fairly McDonald

Coconut Candy

1 coconut — 3 cups sugar

To the coconut juice, add if needed enough sweet milk to fill a cup. Boil this liquid and sugar 6 minutes. Add the fresh coconut meat, shredded or grated, and boil 10 minutes, stirring constantly. Beat until creamy, and drop on buttered marble slab, using two teaspoons for the purpose.

Bessie Teague

Chocolate Fudge

2 c sugar 1 c sweet milk
Piece butter Pinch salt
1 tsp. vanilla ½ c chopped nuts
2 Large sqs. Baker's bitter chocolate
2 tbsp. Marshmallow cream

Put milk, chocolate, and sugar on to cook. Stir well. After it comes to a good boil, add big piece of butter. Then add a pinch of soda, stirring most of the time, so it won't stick to bottom of pan. When it forms a soft ball by dropping some in cold water, remove from fire and add 2 tbsp. marshmallow cream, vanilla, pinch salt, and nuts. Beat until smooth and ready to pour up. Pour on a greased platter.

Mrs. Hilton Price

Orange Cream Candy

Mix 2½ cups sugar with 1 cup milk and cook 'til it forms soft ball when dropped in cold water. Add juice and shredded rind of 1 orange. Cook 'til soft ball stage again. Add 1 tbsp. butter. Cool, beat and add 1 qt. nuts

Mary Oliver McLemore

Pralines

1 cup brown sugar
1 cup white sugar
½ cup confectioner's sugar
½ cup maple syrup
¾ cup rich milk or cream
Pinch of soda — pinch of salt.

Mix and cook 'til soft ball stage. Remove from fire and beat 'til it begins to thicken. Add 2 cups nuts and drop on waxed paper.

Mrs Roy Nolen

Candied Grapefruit

Cut rind of 1 large grapefruit into thin strips. Dissolve 1 Tbsp. salt in 1 qt. water. Add grapefruit and let soak all night. Drain and boil 4 times in different waters. Drain, add 2 cups sugar and cook slowly until dry. When cold, roll in sugar.

                Mrs. George A. Robbins

Sugared Pecans

1½ cups sugar	¼ cup water
3 Tbsp. orange juice	pinch of salt
½ Tsp. grated orange rind	
½ lb. salted pecans	

Cook sugar, water and orange juice until a little dropped in water forms a firm, soft ball. Remove from fire, add nuts and grated rind. Stir until syrup looks cloudy. Try to spread pecans as much as possible.

                Mrs. John Kohn

Pickles and Relishes

Indian Chutney

25 hard green preserving pears
1 lb. raisins   5 lbs. granulated sugar
1 tbs. ground ginger   1 tbs. ground cinnamon
1 tbs. ground cloves   2 small garlic cloves
8 or 10 hot red peppers (small)   1/4 lb. salt
1 1/2 pts. vinegar

Peel and slice pears, grind garlic and peppers fine, mix with spices and salt in a little vinegar — mash well together. Make a syrup of sugar and vinegar. Put everything together and boil 1/2 hour. Seal in jars while hot.

  Dorothy Graham Dedrick
   Maxwell Field, Ala

Fig Preserves

Select 10 lbs. of figs not too ripe. Put fruit in a preserving kettle, with enough water to cover the fruit and let boil 5 minutes. Do not let fruit lose its shape. Drain fruit and return to kettle in layers with sugar, allowing 1 lb. of sugar for each lb. of fruit. Let stand overnight. Next morning place kettle on stove. Cook 2 sliced lemons in a pint of water for 1/2 hr. & add them, with the water, to the figs. Add 2 tbsp of ginger — and cook until syrup is thick.

  Mrs. Loula M. Stone.

Peach Chutney

½ cup chopped onions
½ lb. raisins
1 clove garlic
4 lb. fresh peaches
2 tbsp. red chili powder
⅔ cup chopped crystalized ginger
2 tbsp. mustard seeds
1 tbsp. salt
1 qt. vinegar
1 ¼ lbs. brown sugar

Put raisins, onions, and garlic through food chopper. Peel peaches, cut in small pieces and mix with other ingredients. Boil slowly for fully 1 hr. or until chutney is rich brown color and rather thick. Pack in hot sterilized jars. Makes 3 pts.

Mrs. R. M. Rawlinson,
Millbrook, Alabama

Sweet Peach Pickle

Peel 1 peck peaches and stick whole cloves on each side.

Syrup for peaches
8 cups sugar
4 cups apple vinegar

When syrup boils add peaches. When peaches begin to get tender add 2 tbps. whole allspice and continue cooking until tender. Place a few pieces of whole stick cinnamon in jars. Fill with peaches and cover with juice.

Mrs. Clarence Garric

~ Chili Sauce ~

287-

½ peck skinned ripe tomatoes
3 large green peppers
1 Tbsp. ground cloves   6 large onions
1 Tbsp. ground allspice   2 cups sugar
1 Tbsp. ground cinnamon   4 Tbsps. salt
1 Tbsp. white mustard seed
1 Tbsp. celery seed   1 qt. vinegar

Cut tomatoes, onions and peppers in small pieces. Put on stove with other ingredients and cook until thick enough not to run — about 4 hours.

Louise Mathews —

Chow Chow

Boil separately:
1 qt. lima beans   1 qt small pickling onions
1 qt. little green beans cut short
1 head cauliflower, cut small before boiling
blanche these

Do NOT Cook
1 qt corn cut off cob (about 9 ears)
chop 6 red and 6 green bell peppers
1 qt. (1 pt. will do) of gherkins (sweet)
Make paste of 1/4 lb. Colman's dry mustard and 1/4 lb. White Lily Flour, adding gradually 3 pts. vinegar.
Add to this:
1 lb. sugar   red and black pepper
3 tbs salt   tumeric to color
2 tsp. celery seed

Let all seasoning come to a boil. Put in all raw ingredients and cook a few minutes then **add cooked vegatables** and let boil a short time. Put in jars while hot. Makes 6 qts.

Mrs. William B. Bankhead
Jasper, Alabama

Bread and Butter Pickles

1 qt. dill pickles cut in rings
3 c sugar   1½ c vinegar
1 garlic button   1 tsp. celery seed
1 tbsp. whole allspice   1 stick cinnamon
Dash of black pepper.
Bring all above ingredients to boil. Add drained pickles. Cook until transparent. Pour in fruit jars.

   Mrs. Cliff Green

Crisp Sweet Pickle

2 qts. dill pickle cut in rounds
1 qt. vinegar   5 lb. sugar
1 bud garlic   whole cloves
whole black pepper

Mix all the above ingredients. The second day add 1 cup oil.

Mix in crock and stir every day for a week.

   Mrs. Yetta Samford
   Opelika, Ala.

290. Green Tomato Crystallized Pickle.

7 lbs. green tomatoes. Wash and slice before final weighing. Put in lime water (2 cups lime to 2 gals. water) let stand 24 hours. Wash well. Soak in alum water (¼ lb. or 10¢ box) to 2 gals. water for 24 hrs. Wash well. Soak in ginger water (5¢ box pulverized) to 2 gals. water for 6 hrs. Wash well. Make syrup of 5 lbs. sugar and 3 pts. vinegar with 1 Tsp. each of cinnamon, whole cloves, whole allspice and celery seed. Pour over tomatoes and let stand 4 hrs. Boil 1 hour. Do not have to seal while hot. (This syrup does not cover tomatoes, so, if preferred, cover with vinegar and then use 6 lbs. sugar.) Do not use an aluminum vessel.

~French Pickles

4 lbs. cucumbers   6 pods red bell pepper
2 lbs. onions   1 tbsp. celery seed
½ gal vinegar   2 tbsp. mustard seed
1 qt. sugar   1 oz. tumeric

    Peel and slice cucumbers and onions. Let stay in salt 24 hours. Wash out salt and squeeze out all liquid. Let vinegar and other ingredients come to a boil. Add cucumbers and onions and boil 10 min. When cold add 4 tbsp. olive oil or Wesson oil.

Miss Betty Allen

~Artichoke Pickle

    Rub well with a coarse towel, 1 peck artichokes. Slice, 1 qt. onions. Soak both artichokes and onions in salt water for 3 days, in seperate vessels.

1 gal. vinegar   2 boxes white mustard seed
2 tbsp. mustard   1 box black mustard seed
2 tsp. allspice   6 cups sugar
2 tsp. cloves   enough tumeric to color

    Add onions and boil 5 min. Let this get cold, and pour over artichokes that have been placed in jars. Seal and do not use for a month.

Miss Marjorie Allen

Cabbage Pickle

1 1/2 gallons shredded cabbage sprinkle with salt and let stand 6 hours. Press the water out.

Cut 1 dozen onions fine, pour boiling water over them, let stand, then drain and mix with cabbage. Add 1/2 dozen green peppers, cut fine, 1 cup mustard, 2 cups white mustard seed, 3 Tbsps. turmeric, 3 Tbsps. celery seed, 1 Tbsp. mace, 1/2 Tbsp. of red pepper and 1 Tbsp. ground cinnamon. Mix well. Boil 1/2 gal. vinegar with 1 lb. sugar. Stir the pickle in when it has just begun to boil and stir until it is thoroughly heated. Take off and put in glass jars.

E. P. Flowers —

Pickled Watermelon Rind

Use only white rind of watermelon. Cut in cubes one inch square. Cover with hot water and parboil until it can be pierced with a fork - but be careful not to get it too soft. For 20 cups of rind, make a syrup of 7 cups sugar - 2 cups vinegar - ¼ tsp. oil of cloves - ½ tsp. oil of cinnamon. Bring to a boil and pour over the rind. Let stand overnight. In the morning, pour off the syrup and reheat it. Add again to the rind. Repeat this process for 2 days. On the 3rd day, reheat the rind and the syrup, and seal.

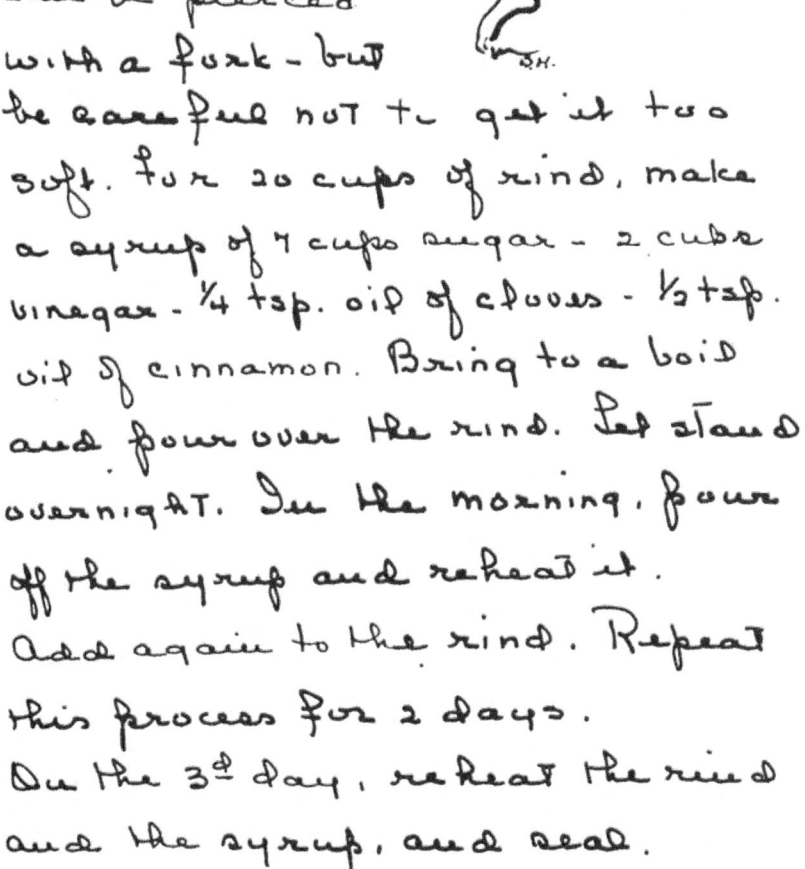

    Mrs. Aubrey Hornsley-

Strawberry Preserves

9 cups sugar   1 cup warm water
        2 qts. strawberries

Cook sugar and water until it crystalizes on spoon. Put berries in and boil hard 15 minutes. Shake boiler while cooking. Pour in large flat pan and shake until cool.

   Mrs. James F. Hegenwald

Blackberry Preserves

5 lbs. berries   5 lbs. sugar

Cap and wipe berries before washing. Put berries in kettle without water and when they begin to simmer, add 1 tsp. soda. When foam rises, skim quickly and add sugar. Boil 20 minutes from time it begins to boil hard. Put in fruit jars and do not seal until cold. Cover with parafin.

   Mrs. James Rice

Spiced Grapes

5 lbs. concord grapes   3 lbs. sugar
1 pt. vinegar   1 tsp. cinnamon
1 tsp. allspice   1 tsp. cloves

Pulp grapes, boil skins until tender in a small quantity of water. Mash pulp good and cook until tender, run through colander, then combine pulp, skins, and other ingredients. Cook slowly like jam.

   Mrs. A. N. Culver

Orange Marmalade

Select clear, fine-grained oranges of a rich color, one orange to one lemon.

Quarter fruit, lay skin side down on wood, and with sharp knife cut across in as thin slices as possible.

Measure 3 cups cold water to each cup sliced fruit; let stand 24 hrs. in crockery or granite container. Next day, cook until skins are very tender, and let stand 24 hrs. again.

Next day, measure 1 c sugar to 1 cup fruit and to every 7th cup add extra cup sugar. Boil briskly until thick white bubbles appear over surface.

Usually 3 large oranges and 3 large lemons are as much as one will care to cut at one time.

When done, let cool 30 min. Stir thoroughly and glass. This keeps fruit from coming to top of glass.

Mrs. G. H. Moore

296-

Blackberry Jelly

Wash berries and mash thoroughly. Let boil 10 minutes and strain. Add 1 cup sugar to 1 cup juice. Cook only 7 cups at a time, adding to this the juice of 1 lemon. Cook rapidly for 30 minutes, skimming while boiling.

— Mrs. George Brackin —

Plum Sauce

Take ½ gallon firm plums, wash and cover with water. Boil 15 minutes. Pour off water, add 2 lbs. sugar and ½ Tea-cup good apple vinegar. Boil ½ hour. Mix ½ Tsp. each extract of cloves and ginger with a little water and add to mixture. Boil for a few minutes, pour up in a jar and seal.

HELP

— Mrs. A. H. Marshall —

For Special Recipes

Tomato Juice Cocktail Supreme

3 cups canned tomatoes
1/2 cup water
2 medium sized onions
2 bay leaves
1 level tsp. salt
1/8 tsp. black pepper
1/4 tsp. catsup
1/4 cup orange juice

Put canned tomatoes into deep stew pan, add water and onions, which have been peeled and cut into thick slices, bay leaves; salt; sugar; pepper; and celery salt. Cook, closely covered, over low flame for 20 min. Strain and add catsup and orange juice. Bottle and let cool.

Mrs. William S. Dawdell

Russian Tea

2 qts. strained tea
2 cups sugar
2 lemons
12 Cloves
3 oranges
1 qt. water

Extract juice from lemons and oranges. Boil rinds and cloves in 1 qt. water for 5 minutes. Strain, add sugar, juices and tea. Serve hot.

Mrs. Noble Seay

Carolina Mint Tea
(Charleston)

2 cups sugar   ½ cup water
1 orange rind (grated)
Juice of 6 oranges
6 glasses very strong Orange Pekoe Tea
Several sprigs mint

Boil sugar, water and orange rind about 5 minutes to make syrup. Remove from fire, add the crushed leaves of mint, let cool. Make the tea, strain and add orange juice. Half fill the glass with crushed ice, add tea and sweeten to taste with the mint syrup. A fresh sprig of mint or a slice of orange in each glass adds to the attractiveness of the drink. Mrs. Oliver Rutledge Jr.

Mint Punch

12 lemons
2 handfuls mint
2½ C sugar
1½ C water

Squeeze lemons. Put juice and rinds in bowl with the mint which has been bruised. Cook sugar and water until thoroughly dissolved. Pour into other mixture. Let cool. Add water.

Mrs. Arthur Mead

Apricat Wine

1 lb. seeded raisins   3 lbs. sugar
1 lb. dried apricots   1 gal water
1 yeast cake (dissolved in a little warm water)

Let stand in covered stone jar a month. Syphon off, strain (with cloth bag) and bottle. Keep 1 year before using. (Muddy part toward bottom will strain clear if run through filter paper)

Mrs. W. B. Nelson

Blackberry Nectar

To 5 oz. of tartaric acid put 2 qts. water. Dissolve and pour over 12 lbs. of berries. Do not mash fruit. Let stand 48 hours. Strain and to 1 pt. juice add 1½ lbs. sugar. Stir lightly. Bottle. Use 1 to 2 tbs. syrup to a glass of crushed ice when serving.

Mrs. C. G. Hume

Peach Bounce

Peel, chop and sweeten a medium sized bowl of soft peaches. Let stand 2 or 3 hours. Make a strong unsweetened lemonade and let stand a short while. Add peach mixture when ready to serve.

Mrs. Henry Habbie, Jr.

Coca Cola Punch

Juice of 1 doz. lemons
3 c. sugar
5 pts. water
Grated lemon rind

Mix and let stand over night. Strain and add 6 Coca Cola or Royal Crown Cola.

Mrs. Sam Helburn

Lemon Cocktail

8 tbsp. water   Rind 1 lemon
1 cup sugar   1 cup cold water
Juice 4 or 6 lemons

Boil 8 tbsp. water, sugar, and lemon rind for 3 min. Remove from stove and add cold water, peppermint drops, and lemon juice. Serve over crushed ice with sprig of mint and cherry.

Mrs. Frank Samford, Birmingham

For Special Recipes

For Special Recipes

For Special Recipes

Made in the USA
Coppell, TX
04 December 2021